# YOUNG LIFE

# YOUNG LIFE

*Emile Cailliet*

HARPER & ROW, PUBLISHERS

NEW YORK, EVANSTON, AND LONDON

To Jim

"Walk in wisdom toward them
that are without . . ."
Colossians 4:5

FIRST EDITION

M-N

LIBRARY OF CONGRESS CATALOG CARD NUMBER: 64-10614

# CONTENTS

# ACKNOWLEDGMENTS

THE TREATMENT AT HAND is derived from personal observations and inquiries dating back to the summer of 1958, when I spent four weeks at the Young Life Graduate Institute, Fountain Valley, Colorado and visited Young Life ranches in the neighboring mountains. Here I first met Jim Rayburn, the originator and executive director of the Young Life Campaign, and Roy R. Riviere, his executive assistant, as well as many others involved in this work. In subsequent years I was the personal guest of Jim Rayburn at Frontier Ranch and Silver Cliff Ranch near Buena Vista, Colorado. There, week after week, I followed closely the activities of one set of teen-agers after another. In Colorado Springs I enjoyed a perfect hospitality at the streamlined headquarters of Young Life, where I had free access to all needed files and documents, including some of a confidential nature.

In addition I have been placed on the mailing list of Young Life workers in the field, a privilege which has allowed me to follow every new development. Personal requests for information or clarification have been promptly satisfied. An active participation in the Young Life Eastern and Southeastern Conference held in Natural Bridge, Virginia in January 1963 has allowed me to come in closer touch with the staff and its leaders, beginning with George Sheffer, regional director for the Southwest, who patiently answered my inquiries. I confess having previously taken advantage of various Colorado gatherings to subject Bob Mitchell, Western regional director, and Bill Starr, Midwestern regional director, to similar questioning. Needless to say, other members of the staff have not escaped interrogation. It has been especially gratifying that most persevering of them all in answering queries has been Jim Rayburn himself.

Facts dating back to the early days of the Campaign have been provided by such men as Addison G. Sewell, a charter member of the Young Life staff. Communications from Mr. Sewell and others have permitted me to get a better perspective on positive and enduring results, as well as on the relevance of my criticism of certain features. Testimony from churchmen such as the Rev. Mynerd Meekhof of Seattle, laymen such as Mr. Charles Duncan of Philadelphia, and especially parents, have opened up new vistas on the impact of Young Life on an average American family.

The records concerning experiences and activities presented in this book have been authenticated by men and women in the field, from executive officers through regional, metropolitan, and area directors to area committee members and local workers—over a hundred in all. Actual names of youngsters, high schools, colleges, and metropolitan areas have in many instances had to be either omitted or deleted, to avoid obvious possibilities of embarrassment or invasion of privacy. It has also seemed advisable to be sparing in the use of names of Young Life leaders involved in special situations. I wish it were possible to mention all those who by their kind and joyful assistance have contributed useful information; I should hate to be guilty of inadvertent omissions. Let those concerned find here the expression of a heartfelt gratitude already conveyed to them personally in private correspondence.

Nor would it be fair to publish this book without acknowledging my debt to the valuable advice of my daughter Doris, of the Harper editorial staff, of Annabel Learned, and especially to the tireless patience and painstaking care of Mrs. Paul H. Burton in typing and retyping the manuscript.

EMILE CAILLIET

*Cape May, New Jersey*

# INTRODUCTION

Teen-agers are not popular in America today.

Shortly after my return from Frontier Ranch, one of the strategic centers of the Young Life Campaign in the Colorado mountains, a Salvation Army truck stopped in front of my house for the usual collection of old newspapers and discarded articles. Glad to find the door open, the collector cheerfully asked me where I had been.

"Why, I've been at a summer camp with a lot of teen-agers," I explained.

His face took on a stern expression as he commented, "I feel sorry for you."

Had I been wise, I would have drawn in my mind some kind of dividing line between the chance utterance of this good man and the considered pronouncement of a trained officer. In truth, the remark of the Salvation Army aid did not reflect the well-known position of the organization. Yet on the spur of the moment that did not occur to me. As the man went on with his work, I could not help pondering the plight of our youngsters.

"Even a Salvation Army man," I found myself saying. "Even a Salvation Army man!"

By then the truck had pulled out of the driveway, but an aching sense of loneliness somehow lingered. Suddenly the thought came to

1

me with more convincing power than ever before: But Young Life is there! There to befriend the youngsters on the athletic field, in the corner drugstore, at the high-school play—there to win their confidence, in the fullness of time their friendship—there to deliver them from their fear and prejudices, at least long enough to allow them to take an intelligent look at the Christ and to decide for themselves whether or not to acknowledge his claims for their lives.

From obscure beginnings in 1940, when Jim Rayburn befriended high-school students in three Texas cities, the Young Life Campaign has penetrated wide areas in more than thirty states and Canada. It is gaining ground overseas, with initial progress in France and Germany. Expansion to South America beginning with Brazil is now under consideration. At this time of writing, over 220 devoted and at least college-trained men and women, helped by a student staff, plus 500 volunteer leaders and 900 committee members, affect the lives of thousands upon thousands of teen-agers. And yet, to this day there has not been a single comprehensive introduction of Young Life to the public at large, to the youngsters themselves, and to their parents and teachers.

This small volume is aimed to fill that gap, at least temporarily. The firsthand research on which it is based, especially with reference to American teen-agers, may prove valuable to researchers in the field, whatever their own views on the relevance of the Young Life Campaign per se. The hundreds of well-authenticated facts and events here brought together will, it is hoped, provide solid material.

My own interest in Young Life was awakened by the fact that here was a company of persons who, instead of lamenting the plight of our teen-agers, were doing something about it. It may also be that a man in his late sixties experiences increasingly that mysterious affinity between the old and the young which has found such wonderful expression in Victor Hugo's *The Art of Being a Grandfather*. Possibly, too, having as a college professor freely indulged in the writing of philosophical treatises, I have felt a certain debt to my fellow man, an obligation to do something practical when the chance offered.

From the outset and all along it has been understood that I was entirely on my own in the undertaking: that is, that I should proceed as I saw fit, without any kind of interference on the part of Young Life representatives. This book is accordingly not a one-sided apology for the movement by a writer swept off his feet by enthusiasm, or worse still, by the prospect of personal advantage. Quite the contrary! What is said in these pages goes beyond description to evaluation, even a critical one.

Young Life leaders, including Jim Rayburn, are the first to admit that after a quarter of a century of advance a reassessment of aims, tactics, and strategy is in order, if not somewhat overdue. Hence any criticism loses its sting; it is not made, moreover, in a spirit of negativism, but rather by way of gentle warning or would-be-helpful suggestion. It could hardly be otherwise, if this book is to reflect the spirit of Young Life itself—that of a God-given friendship.

Written in the awareness that the Young Life movement strikingly mirrors the personal experience, outlook, and evangelical concern of its founder and executive director, Jim Rayburn, the following pages open with a biographical account of the facts and events that brought the Campaign into existence. The main body of the volume shows Young Life at work on campuses, at weekend and summer camps, and in slum areas. A brief and highly condensed presentation of case studies here and there throughout the volume suggests the subsequent renewal of youth in a glow of faith and hope, while the final chapters take a forward look at the tasks of tomorrow.

As I pondered the Salvation Army aid's remark that day, I had a vivid recollection of Jim Rayburn at prayer. This man who originated the Young Life movement and has been its living inspiration through the years is one of the most unassuming, most revered leaders of our day and age. The picture of Jim I then so clearly remembered was not connected with one of those Young Life camp gatherings when the crowd of youngsters noisily greet the appearance of their beloved chief. There had been an interlude of a few days at Frontier Ranch, between batches of vacationing teen-agers, to allow for a national meeting of local committee representatives. In each community where there is a Young Life program, there is a committee of businessmen responsible for promotion and support of the program and staff in that area. As noted above, about 900 committee members are at present officially listed. The national gathering it had been my privilege to attend was of necessity a sober, matter-of-fact kind of meeting, essentially concerned with budget-framing and other matters affecting work at the local level. It was at one of the regular evening sessions that I saw Jim Rayburn at prayer as I later recalled him.

There was Jim, standing at a small desk which at his insistence had been set up at the floor level rather than on a podium high above the delegates. His ruddy, infinitely kind face was lifted up, its features sharply outlined in light and shadow, very much like a Rembrandt portrait. The cares and deep concern of a fully committed life were writ deep in lines and furrows that gave his expression a weather-beaten appearance, like a man who in any kind of circumstances stood ready to submit to the Lord's will for the sake of the one thing that mattered.

Good Lord, give us the teen-agers, that we may lead them to thee. Our hearts ache for the nine million young people who remain untouched by thy Gospel, and for the tragically large proportion of those who, having once been led to attend Sunday school, have dropped by the wayside and now find themselves without spiritual guidance. Help us give them a chance, O Father, a chance to become aware of thy Son's beauty and healing power in the might of the Holy Spirit. O Lord Jesus, give us the teen-agers, each one at least long enough for a meaningful confrontation with thee. We are at best unprofitable servants, but thy grace is sufficient. O thou, Holy Spirit, give us the teen-agers, for we love them and know them to be awfully lonely . . . Good Lord, give us the teen-agers!

Jim's whole being was in that prayer. When he had finished, his thin, muscular body was leaning forward in vibrant self-offering. His face, radiant with love, continued to pray long after his lips had closed, as if what he had to say could no longer be put into words. What an ineffable experience his prayer was that evening! I shall always find it inseparable from my thought of Young Life.

The work of the Young Life Campaign among people of high-school age is not motivated by such considerations as immediately concern the civil authorities charged with maintaining law and order among our often troubled young people. Its prime mover is love, the kind of love that only the God who was in Christ can inspire. Hence the phrase "personal friendship evangelism," often used to characterize the Young Life approach to teen-agers. The movement is not to be used, still less exploited or controlled, by state or local agencies who are at grips with delinquency problems and swelling budgets. It is out to reach the youngsters and make them aware of their God-given opportunity to hear about a life-changing truth, accessible in and through the person and work of Jesus Christ—aware of their right of choice, once the confrontation has taken place.

What the Young Life leadership has long realized is that only the understanding of love on the part of adults will allow useful communication with adolescents. The first step in this understanding of love, as the leaders see it, must be a candid acknowledgment of a youngster's status and dignity as a human being originally created in the image of God. Communication, far from being equated with indoctrination, implies listening, learning, discovering. It then appears that a younster's propensity for rebellion is to be ascribed first of all to his being young. His disparagement of adults, beginning with parents, is of the same origin. Jim Rayburn likes to point out that if you have a child who goes through his adolescent years praising you to the sky, you had better take him to a psychiatrist.

Naturally defiant of authority or power assumed by adults, teen-agers *are* often pronounced ungovernable, and their spirit rebellious to the point of violence and outrage. These and other judgments reach full expression in the phrase "juvenile delinquency" with all its implications. Let it be freely granted that none should shut his eyes to occasional collective debasement among young people, or to the wanton damage that appears in its wake (yet even such a painful expression should be met with the reasonableness that only a genuine, loving concern can express). This once said—and it must be said— the diagnosis of juvenile delinquency to a large extent exposes the failure of adults adequately to evaluate adolescence.

For adolescence is not a mere season of growth from puberty to maturity, nor simply a period of transition between childhood and manhood or womanhood. It is an age of its own—on its own, and mostly all its own. The teen-agers' landscape of reality has its particular features. It is a new world which develops its own ways of doing and thinking, its customs, its appropriate language—in fact, some of that wisdom unaware of itself which we adults call tradition. In this exclusive world of the teen-ager each generation stands ready to fight afresh its war of independence. It need not surprise anyone, therefore, that the Young Life movement, one of the first to give full recognition and status to the rising generation, should have been initiated in America—a new world itself not so long ago.

# 1

# CHALLENGE TO HIGH
# ADVENTURE

*A Decisive Call*

PASCAL HAS POINTED OUT THAT, in writing a book, the last thing we discover is what to put first. But I am sure I know how to begin, for what has impressed me most in my study of Young Life is the overwhelming sense of the sovereignty of God which inspires all its activities. Young Life leaders would never think of taking credit for any success they may achieve. To them it is God who does it all. From one moment to another they trustingly and expectantly wonder what he will do next. Ever prompt at self-effacement, they watch for the providential ways in which he controls the course of events and directs it toward the purpose of his will. They are convinced that the thing for them to do is to try to make out the meaning of whatever comes to pass. Their relation to the Lord is the center of their existence.

Moreover, the extent to which this Young Life point of view reflects the outlook and experience of Jim Rayburn, founder of the movement, is truly amazing. Going forth to find spiritually unreached young people and to let them discover for themselves a holy purpose in their lives, Jim Rayburn became involved, touched others, started a lifelong career. Hence an essential clue to any real understanding of the Young Life movement must be looked for in the experience of its originator, as he found himself challenged to high adventure.

The sequence of events that brought Young Life into existence and continues to keep it aglow with a tremendous vitality began in the days following the great depression of 1929. Without much conviction, Jim had studied engineering at Kansas State University and then mineralogy at the University of Colorado Graduate School. He was haunted by the example of his Presbyterian father, whose life-work had been evangelism. Finally, in 1933 Jim and his young bride Maxine found their way to the remote southern region of Arizona and New Mexico as Presbyterian home missionaries.

During their three opening years of service, the couple's happiest results were obtained among young people. Acknowledgment of this fact on Jim's part came much later, but even at the beginning there may have been a foretaste of things to come. What for the moment seems to a man insignificant or mere coincidence, in the fullness of time is found to be part and parcel of a meaningful texture of events. Thus far, Jim's awareness of his work had been limited to a sense of doing the right thing to the best of his knowledge. He conscientiously went through the motions required by a demanding task. His youthful zeal notwithstanding, he was very much on his own. What he lacked, as he now looks back upon this period, was a sense of the Presence of God. The heavenly Seeker would soon arouse this sense in him amid the most ordinary, everyday circumstances. Truly the living God of the Bible is the great Doer of the unexpected.

One afternoon on an Arizona camping trip, Jim found his way to a ghost town. There he came upon a scuffed, coverless copy of *He That Is Spiritual*, by Lewis Sperry Chafer—the "evangelist without a method," as he came to be known. With a strange feeling of satisfaction, Jim slipped the book into his pocket and hurried back to his home quarters to read it. Hardly had he begun than one fact emerged from the dusty pages: the Spirit-filled Christians are the only ones to enjoy the blessings of genuine liberty. Chafer claimed that the divine leading does not set down rules. What is expected of a

Christian is commitment, utter reliance upon Providence. Surrender fully to the Lord and you will know what heavenly guidance means.

As Jim went rapidly from one page to the next, a new life dimension seemed to come within range. What increasingly dawned upon him was that to have been converted, and accordingly to have become a Christian, is one thing; yet for this same Christian to become genuinely spiritual is another. Only the fullness of the Spirit could bring the certainty of revelation to the soul. With this certainty came freedom and power, the power that makes one mighty in and through prayer. Let the Spirit of Life dwell in a man, permeate his being, sanctify his nature, quicken his faculties, vitalize his mortal body, and this man will live—really live! He will live the life that is life indeed.

The shadows were lengthening. It was getting dark. Their household budget did not yet allow for the luxury of a lamp, so Jim lit a candle. By its flickering light he spent the whole night reading, his wife's protests notwithstanding. He was convinced that this providentially discovered book was *for him!* Chafer's basic assertion spoke to Jim's condition: "A Christian is a Christian because he is rightly related to Christ; but 'he that is spiritual' is spiritual because he is rightly related to the Spirit, in addition to his relation to Christ in salvation." Up to this time, Jim had known himself to be related to Christ in salvation, but he had not known what it meant to be rightly related to the Spirit. And here, as he bent over the poorly lit page, this very Spirit was contending with him—no longer as an abstract doctrine, no longer as an *it*, but as *he* who bears witness to Christ in the soul. Henceforth Jim would yield to that living reality, be molded into the fit instrument that would evermore adequately work in him the purposes of God. He would let himself be restrained, reproved, regenerated, indwelt, baptized afresh, filled with the Power which comes with the Presence, sealed with the seal that identifies the Blessed One.

Physically, Jim is a man of small stature, though his deceptively slight frame is full of vigor, as anyone who tries to follow him on a mountain trail will soon find out. Picture this frail-looking young man on his knees as the light of his candle faded away in the dawn of a new day. The great Seeker had found him. Jim was endued and the Spirit was clothed.

The young man expected the Lord to disclose to him there and then the nature and extent of his divine purpose; but in vain. Jim soon understood that this could never be God's way for one who had "become spiritual." He would not be given a blueprint for his life, to be slipped into his pocket and carried around with him. Quite the contrary. The heavenly Father wanted him to grow into a loving dependence upon the Spirit, to foster in his whole being an utter trust in his Providence. The only thing Jim was given to know before he left his Arizona station was his own immediate need for special education which would allow him to proceed with his God-assigned task, whatever it might prove to be. With this realization, he made the decision to seek full seminary training. A Philadelphia church which had supported the young couple in Arizona agreed to contribute sixty dollars a month toward their upkeep.

With all their possessions packed, Jim and Maxine left the scene of their first labors on an expedition that proved to be a journey in faith in the tradition of Abraham the Hebrew, the man from the other side who had been dwelling in a tent because he looked for a city. As they began their trip they were still undecided whether it would lead to San Francisco Seminary or Dallas Seminary. God's covenant with them had been a one-sided covenant, just as with Abraham. The glory of it was that he who made the covenant was a covenant-keeping God. Now, in his hands and at his mercy, they were safe, their faith grounded in his utter trustworthiness. They could depend on him for the next step. In this blessed assurance they reached the fork where the highway branched off east and west. There they stopped their car and prayed, asking God in what direction he would have them turn. They turned east.

Jim began his studies at the Dallas Seminary in the fall of 1936. Before his Arizona experience everyday happenings had not made much sense to him, but during his first year at seminary he exulted in being able for the first time to read the script of his own life as it unrolled.

Like every seminary student, he had to find his place in the field education program in order to acquire the basic skills of a minister of the Gospel. While his supervised training on the field was planned to give him diversified opportunities for observation and study, it happened to emphasize youth leadership in a Dallas church.

To promote child evangelism in that church Jim organized "Good News" clubs in the name of the Gospel. He had his boys' club as well, of which the member best known in later years was Doak Walker, all-time football great from Southern Methodist University. This was to be the pattern of Jim's first two seminary years—assistant to the pastor and youth leader. What proved infinitely more rewarding to him than the five dollars a week compensation he received (actually paid only about ten times) was the increasing assurance that the Lord's will for him was pointing to a ministry among teen-agers.

## The Young Life Club Idea

In the fall of 1938, the young seminarian's field work program brought him face to face with a man of vision who became, unawares, the herald of God's will for the Young Life Campaign. This was the minister of the Presbyterian Church in Gainsville. His assignment to Jim (again assistant and youth leader) was unique. A program had already been provided for the teen-agers who came to church. "Jim," the minister explained, "I'm not particularly worried about the kids who are in. They're safe, and as far as they're concerned I don't need your services. To you I entrust the crowd of teen-agers who stay away from church. The center of your widespread parish will be the local high school."

The good man had no way of realizing at the time how farsighted and ultimately far-reaching this charge would prove to be. Yet this much was obvious: it was a New Testament-centered assignment, embodying the basic element of Christ's commission: "Go ye . . ." In practice, Jim had found the "Come ye" type of invitation more congenial to the clergy. And yet those who serve the great Seeker should themselves be seekers. One of the reasons some nine million teen-agers remain beyond the influence of churches today is that too many ministers restrict themselves to meeting high-school students in church or having them partake in church-structured activities. As a result, a minister seldom sees teen-agers in their own environment. He limits his acquaintance, and possibly that of an assistant, to the way they look and behave on Sunday.

What is further at fault in this approach is that it reflects an understanding of the word "church" which is not found in the New Testament—namely, as a building used for public worship rather than as a group of dedicated people, seeking others wherever they may be found. There is in the Christian tradition no known reference to a church building before the second century. The first-century gatherings of Christians were actually held in the private houses of those concerned, as may be seen in Romans 16:5, I Corinthians 16:19, Colossians 4:15, and Philemon 2. For Jim, the recovery of this New Testament outlook was at hand. He was led to acknowledge as his key Bible verse Colossians 4:5: "Walk in wisdom toward them that are without . . ." He could hardly have foreseen the amount of exertion and trial and error implied in working out the wisdom mentioned in this New Testament passage. But it is just and right that God never does for us what we are able to do by ourselves.

In that fall of 1938, Jim found that to reach teen-agers for Christ was more easily said than done. Was the Gainsville Presbyterian minister joking when he said that Jim's center of operation was to be the local high school and his parishioners the young crowd that did not come to church? How should he go about such an assignment? Jim had once heard of an organization called the Miracle Book Club, so he borrowed the name and started a Miracle Book Club of his own. It met once a week after school in a classroom. An average of ten youngsters attended from winter through spring to the next fall, yet results proved disappointing. Jim looked hard for books on youth work, but found none of the kind he needed. He held himself ready to be taught, but there were no teachers to instruct him in what he wanted to know. Seminaries are more involved with theological questions than with the details of teen-age evangelism. Who could tell him, for example, how to deal with a group of boys holding girls on their laps? Yet this was the kind of thing he encountered from the very beginning, which was to plague him for a long time.

In January of 1940, a nagging uneasiness made him think that there must be a better way to capture the attention and loyalty of high-school students than through a Miracle Club that worked no miracle. And so it was that he hit upon a new conception of what a club for teen-agers should be. It dawned on him that the time at which a meeting was scheduled had to be selected in terms of teen-agers' value conflicts. From this angle, it became obvious that a meeting held just after classes amounted to a scholastic tail end at which a "real guy" would be sure to turn thumbs down. But fix a meeting for, say, 7:30 P.M. and the whole affair takes on a new look. Likewise, if the meeting takes place away from school premises it will seem more like an adult occasion, and the teen-agers will feel they are invited to a social affair of their own instead of just another extracurricular activity for sissies and "squares." That teen-agers are self-conscious about how they regard themselves and what others think of them is a truism—which explains, for example, why defects of complexion or dress constitute a major problem. But let some attractive young fellow show up, and along they go with a whoop and a holler!

In order to establish useful communication with these teens, therefore, Jim resolved to accept their language, preferences, peculiarities, ways of thinking, and so on; to familiarize himself with their tradition, share their values, learn to speak their vernacular, and somehow move into their understanding. A new world of possibilities opened up to him as he reassessed the task before him.

He decided that the meeting should be moved to a house across the street and a new kind of program devised, which might progressively develop the essentials of a successful youth organization. The idea of what has since become the Young Life Club was taking shape. A group of ten or twelve boys attended the first meeting, but the following week twenty-two were present. What a surprise this was— what a triumph! Yet it was just the beginning, for during the remaining sixteen weeks of the school year every meeting improved on the preceding one, until at the last one 175 youngsters assembled.

More significant than this increase in attendance were the spiritual results of this first "campaign." The attention of some of the originally uninterested teen-agers had been captured long enough for a thoughtful consideration of Christ. Although no pressure of any kind was exerted, quite a few genuine conversions had taken place. To be sure, there had been in the early days evidence of scornful mirth and a prolonged testing of Jim by outrageous behavior. He apparently came through it, in the end, with flying colors, for a nucleus of more respectful youngsters took shape. One of these, a huge football player, even became his self-appointed bodyguard.

"Any fellow who makes trouble for Jim will have to lick me first," he pronounced. In the long run, a higher loyalty was called forth among these lively, sometimes wild young people—loyalty to Christ.

What the youngsters seemed to appreciate most was the regard for their personal dignity as human beings; the fact that no pressure had been brought to bear by the leader. All along, their right of choice had been respected, even while the opportunity of confrontation and the Lord's claim to their loyalty were faithfully presented to them. This was a good deal, they thought.

## Two Temptations Resisted

So strongly knit was the original Gainsville nucleus of Christian teen-agers that it seems as if God had used it to preserve the integrity of the movement then in the making. Two temptations were likely to affect its identity—the efforts of churches trying to annex Jim, and the real danger of reverting to outmoded forms of evangelism current in the area. Let us briefly examine these points, for—as will later be seen—they have not lost their relevance in our day.

Jim Rayburn's success had caught the attention of several churches struggling with the problem of teen-age attendance. It was most natural for them to try to secure the services of a young man well on his way to a solution. When he graduated from seminary that spring he received a number of offers. Lewis S. Chafer, author of the very book God had used to set Jim's feet on the path of his life journey, and whom by this time he had come to know, strongly encouraged his young disciple to accept the ministry of a church. Great was the temptation to heed so qualified a voice. Yet, on the other hand, the Gainsville teen-agers to whom he had shown the Lord wanted Jim to stay with them. Quite a few had been genuinely converted, and these now wanted their parents to be led to Christ. They reasoned that Jim had begun the work and ought to see it through. They needed him.

The final decision was not due to any lack of profound reverence for the Church on Jim's part. He was indeed in a dilemma, for he found himself essentially on his own. The youngsters he was chiefly after—those untouched by any knowledge of Christ—stayed carefully and stubbornly away from churches. Although most of those who now dedicate themselves to Christ do join a church, this is usually *after* the club experience. He had discovered, also, a certain proportion of youngsters who had begun by attending church—were, in fact, nominally Christian—but with the impatience of modern, restless youth had become easily bored with the program and had finally left.

It is fair, perhaps, to say that what may appear rude and provocative to call "boredom" on their part (although they felt it so, with dreadful keenness), was in fact their great need for vital Christian contact in their own terms and tempo, their own language, answering to their own sense of their problems and the modern confusion of the world. Most of all, they needed personal human contact with which they could be at ease. It is, perhaps, merely one of the countless instances in history of human problems momentarily piling up and outstripping our means of dealing with them. The Church, as it was, was incomprehensible to these youngsters as Jim first met them. They simply would not go. But now some of them had seen a wonderful light, and were eager for their families to see it. Yet an initially formal, conventional approach would be of little use here either, with those already fixed in an unchurched pattern of life.

Realizing that the claim of these young people could not be ignored, in June 1940 Jim brought together a temporary board of directors. As he likes to express it, he became an organization in order to stay with the kids. Actually, he had rediscovered the Pauline tradition of local bodies of Christians, and of even smaller bodies of Christians within them, called out as the people of God—the *ekklesia* of the Lord.

The board members, aside from himself, were Lewis S. Chafer, John E. Mitchell, and Ted Benson. Ted, who worked at the seminary, had told a friend, H. J. Taylor of Chicago, about Jim and his activities. Taylor invited Jim to Chicago to outline his plans, and then offered to supply automobile expenses of the new organization for a year. Jim made no provision for salary. Both he and, later, his fellow workers would be entirely faith missionaries. Then the organization would live up to the terms of the original call Jim had experienced at the time of his decision in Arizona. Thanks to the Gainsville teenagers he had led to Christ, he had not allowed himself to be drafted by any presbytery or body of elders. He would not be absorbed by religious organizations already set in their ways. Under God, he was definitely on his own; his work would keep its identity.

The second temptation from which Jim was to be protected was the chance of reverting, at least in part, to currently accepted methods of popular evangelism. In the tradition of the time and in line with the heritage of evangelical groups, a certain conformity was expected of him. He was a youth evangelist, to be sure, yet nonetheless an evangelist. The recollection of his boyhood experiences with his father added to the attraction of hallowed practices. These older ways emphasized forceful, if not aggressive, preaching—the climactic call to the penitential platform, or some kind of exhorting and pleading aimed at "a decision for Christ." Already Jim had come to see that this kind of procedure could only antagonize teen-agers. It would surely have been out of place with the youth group that met week after week in Gainsville. Were things going to be different, now that he was to travel and hold meetings with young people he had never met before? How was he to approach disinterested youngsters who did not know him? How was he to broach his subject at the summer tent meetings just then planned by the temporary board of directors?

At least such meetings would not be single dramatic occasions, but would be held in series, which would allow time for "get-acquainted" periods and help to open channels of communication. There would be singing—but not that "last verse if no one else comes" kind of invitation hymn. Rather it would be cheerful singing, displaying the same state of heart and mind that exalted William Tyndale, as long ago as the year 1525, in his Prologue to the New Testament. For the Gospel still is

. . . good, mery glad and joyful tydings, that maketh a mannes hert glad, and maketh hym synge, daunce and leep for joye.

Here was the singing of joy that should prove wholly adequate as an opening to a series of summer tent meetings for teen-agers.

After a time, Jim hit upon the idea of taking along a quintet of Gospel singers. One of them, Murray Smoot, wrote a song called "Life Begins at Calvary," which is still sung to an old melody in Young Life Clubs today. Later the men themselves thought of adding to their singing some sketches, improvisation, and dialogue. These performances by Jim's singers were meant as a prelude to the presentation of some aspect of the Gospel story. Nevertheless the resulting programs eventually attained professional quality. Although far from an authority in the matter, I shall not forget the performances of trios of men such as Bob Mitchell, Phil McDonald, and Dick Lowey at Frontier Ranch and Silver Cliff Ranch in Colorado. Enriched as they were by skits and jokes in perfectly good taste, these "floor shows," as they were known among the teen-agers themselves, left upon all present the impression that there is such a thing as clean fun, and that Christian living need never be a long-faced affair. It is not hard to see why the entertainment crew won a place in the overall activities of Young Life.

The very name of the movement, Young Life Campaign, was an aftermath of those early series of tent meetings for young people. Trying to think of a designation for the meetings, Taylor hit upon this title, which he had heard as the name of an English youth association.

Permission for its adoption was obtained from the English group.

And so Young Life was incorporated in Texas on October 16, 1941. The full-time staff then consisted of Jim together with four recent seminary graduates who had been won over to his approach and were eager to work with him. These were Wally Howard, George Cowan, Gordon Whitelock, and Addison G. Sewell, whose wife—née Loveta Murphy—had been one of Jim's first converts at the Gainsville club.

Another young man who later became a leader in the movement came from these early East Texas days. Roy Riviere had been befriended as a high-school junior by Add Sewell, and with two or three others had sparked Add's club for several years. After graduating from college, going through military service, and completing his theological training, Roy joined the staff of the Campaign and is now regional director for the Southeast, having served many years as executive assistant at headquarters.

Tom Raley was a carefree, rather wild and undisciplined teen-ager when, like so many others, he came under Add Sewell's influence in those days. Having met Christ, he lovingly submitted to his kingly rule. After college, military service, and seminary training, he too joined the Campaign staff. Currently Northwest regional director and a dynamic Christian leader, he has become one of the most highly regarded guides of the younger generation.

Out of the same background came Tom Bade, another great leader of youth in America today whom we shall meet in these pages. He was the son of parents of German extraction who were nominal Christians, practically unidentified with the Church. Tom hardly cut an impressive figure when Add Sewell met him as a high-school junior. But he responded to the Young Life challenge and made a Christian profession the following spring. Having developed special abilities as an entertainer during the summer, he used them to promote the rapid growth of the Young Life Club at Maine Township High School. Throughout his college days he kept up his activity in Young Life circles. There he met his wife, who during her sophomore year in college had become a Christian through the Campaign's influence. Tom excels in firing the enthusiasm of youth as a comedian and entertainer. An adroit leader and gifted speaker as well, he knows instinctively how to assess rightly both the timing and the wording of the Christian message he has all along been aiming to present.

Thus out of this early period of activity in one small area of East Texas emerged, under the influence of Add Sewell, three of the most effective missionaries to high-school youngsters. These three, moreover, are seen against the background of a large number of others whose record, in many cases, turns out almost as impressive. The influence of these early converts is still being felt.

In truth, Jim and his valiant band had been baptized with the Holy Spirit, and with fire.

# 2

# THE UPWARD TRAIL

## Trusting God

FROM HUMBLE BEGINNINGS—from one man's faltering efforts to reach youngsters for Christ and from his association with like-minded workers in the Lord's vineyard—Young Life came into existence. Pervading it, inspiring all its activities, was and is a sustained belief in the sovereignty of God. It is noteworthy that the mystery involved here is never allowed by Young Life leaders to degenerate into any sort of problem—theoretical or practical. Jim Rayburn and his followers are more prompt than the average theologian to admit that personal faith in divine guidance implies a miraculous element—namely, that Almighty God actually works out his will through human agencies in "off-schedule" ways. To Young Life leaders any attempt to reduce the Lord's rule to natural explanations of the world and its essential physical structure amounts to a glaring denial of New Testament Christianity.

In the Book of Acts there is not a single event later acknowledged to be decisive that is presented as happening in a purely incidental way. Rather, every such event, especially in the life of the Apostle Paul, is seen in a setting of obedience; that is, of determination on the part of those concerned to do the Lord's will. According to John, further guidance is dependent on sustained obedience (John 3:21). Only he who "does the truth"—a pungent Hebrew phrase—is said to come to the light. No wonder Jim's enterprises express the faithfulness of a covenant-abiding walk! The glorious counterpart of dependence on the Lord's will appears in Jim's belief in the relevance of the decisions he has made, as well as his liberation from coercive control by organizations already rigid in their procedures. Indeed, the central, enduring aspect of the philosophy of Young Life presupposes the identity and integrity of the self as a covenant partner with the living God.

Anyone who has decided to live and move and have his being in a firm, uncompromising reliance upon God must expect to be severely tested at practically every step of the way. It was as though God subjected Jim and his fellow pioneers to conditions that would put them on their mettle, rouse them to the measure of their ultimate trust. In 1940, the year before the Young Life Campaign was incorporated, the Rayburns faced the most severe testing of their assurance that God was directing them into a full-time mission to teen-agers.

For a long while they had had no regular income except when Jim worked at an outside job. He and Maxine now had two small daughters to care for. One night at dinner, Maxine told Jim that there was enough formula for Sue's ten o'clock feeding, but nothing for the 2:00 A.M. one and not a penny to buy it with. Neither of them knew what to do. They were just a young couple trying to learn to trust God. They could borrow a half-dollar from some student at school, but somehow it did not seem the right thing. So they prayed together, and Jim went out to a training class for volunteer leaders. After the meeting a young woman who worked with girls in the Dallas slums handed him a tiny paper bag. It contained an offering the girls had saved for him: sixty-seven cents. At an all-night icehouse he bought canned milk for the early feeding.

In the fall of that same year the convenient seminary apartment was no longer available. To make matters worse, the few sources of income expected at that time completely vanished. Jim consulted Dr. Harvey Farmer, famed for his missionary work in North Africa, about the prospect of moving into a house with the lowest possible rent. Dr. Farmer thundered, "Jim, who do you work for?" and proceeded to advise a decent home with decent furnishings that would demonstrate how God cared for his servants. His words galvanized Jim's faith and conviction to the point of renting a home for $40 a month. Where the money would come from he had not the slightest idea. In subsequent fact, the rent was provided by a monthly miracle, and with it untold early lessons in dependence on God. Many similar lessons of trust were learned and continue to be learned by most of the staff workers of Young Life.

Providing for elementary material needs was a severe testing which became inseparable from the need for expansion of the program. The original staff of five men led by Jim had moved west, south, and east from Gainesville and Dallas. Some of them had five clubs meeting every week. Their salary was a hundred dollars a month—when money was available. There was about the whole venture an awe-inspiring simplicity and directness. The pioneers had no organization upon which to rely—they relied on God. There was no guaranteed future, but there was the present moment to be spent in Christ's service. They brought faith and hard work to bear on a missionary frontier.

## New Dimensions

Before turning to a closer view of Young Life activity itself, it may not be inappropriate to outline briefly the scope to which this undertaking of faith has ultimately reached. In order to widen their outreach the staff began to issue a magazine, the first number of which appeared in March 1944. Young Life was an attempt to capture the purpose and energy of the Campaign, to report its direction and plans, to introduce its people and program, and to reflect its work with young moderns. It began as an eight-page leaflet and within two years grew to twenty-eight pages. During 1954 it hit a peak circulation of 13,000. When Orien Johnson became editor in October 1956, the magazine office was moved from Dallas to Colorado Springs and the publication enlarged to thirty-two pages and changed from letter press to offset, making possible a wider range of color and more photos. The best of these were provided in later years by Rudy Vetter, an outstanding art photographer and a man who loves to credit Young Life with the glow of his Christian career. After a number of moves, the magazine came to be edited and laid out at headquarters. This proved a wise step, for it had become an essential part of the Campaign's expansion.

A change in editorial policy that took place in 1961 is a good case in point. The initial aim of *Young Life* had been to say in print what the Young Life Club leader said in person, and to present through fiction, articles, and messages the Christian outlook on life. Through a staff questionnaire in the spring of 1961, it became evident that the actual function of the magazine had gradually changed from one of instruction of Christians and proclamation to non-Christians, to that of promotion. Its most effective use was to demonstrate the work to parents and other adults. It had therefore to be adapted to this increasingly promotional character. Conversely, efforts were made to add adult subscribers and provide them with better information about the ever expanding work of the Young Life Campaign. By this time Jim and his co-workers had a great deal to say on the subject.

The pace of expansion had considerably increased over the years. By 1946 the staff had grown to twelve men and eight women in Dallas, Tyler, Houston, Memphis, Tulsa, Chicago, Seattle, Portland, Bellingham, Yakima, and Mexico. Jim himself was now speaking at some 150 high-school assemblies every year, and the budget had risen to $73,700. At this time a fresh dimension in the expanding Campaign was introduced—the use of volunteer leaders consisting of college students and young business and professional people. Volunteer leaders were first added at Wheaton College in 1946.

Jim had flown many times to the Windy City to lay the groundwork for this innovation. At a time when war restrictions made civilian air travel practically impossible, he surprised even airline authorities by the regularity of his trips. One day an official asked him point-blank, "How do you always manage to get a reservation, or even a last-minute seat, when so many executives in the higher brackets can't—

unless, of course, they're on some kind of official business?"

Jim smiled and then quietly explained, "Sir, you and your officials now under government authority think you are all-powerful because you control the airways and own the planes. Yet none of your planes could fly if it were not for the air."

As the executive looked confused, Jim added with a chuckle: "You see, it's like this: I happen to serve the One who owns the air, and *he* takes care of me!" Whereupon he boarded still another plane.

The work had been fully developed along the lines we have seen, and the Young Life Club had indeed proved to be a real opportunity to present the Gospel to teen-agers. A typical meeting lasted for about an hour, was held on a week night, and was open to any member of the student body of a particular high school who wished to attend. It was held under trained leadership and was painstakingly tailored to teen-age concepts. Its sole purpose was to introduce teen-agers to Christ, and to the wonder of being rightly related to him.

We should note here also the Campaigners, smaller groups of club members who through the ministry of Young Life have become Christians, or are already Christians, and have agreed to study, pray, and have fellowship together. This group is the key to the Young Life Club. Its members constitute the leader's lifeline to other young people. A club is often a success or a failure depending on the dedication of its Campaigners.

## The Camping Program

The expansion of the Young Life staff, the extension of its influence through volunteer leaders, and the branching out of the Campaign in every direction created an ever more pressing need for camping facilities. The leasing of private and state park camps for a week or two of summer conferences did not begin to suffice for the growing demands. The board had begun to talk about a permanent site in the Rocky Mountains. With this, a new phase of guidance for Young Life was at hand.

In the spring of 1946 Jim located a piece of property near Colorado Springs called Crystal Park. H. J. Taylor of Chicago, who had been a strong advocate of a Young Life camp, was persuaded to come from Chicago to see it. From then on a bewildering sequence of events emphasized afresh what Jim and his followers had felt all along, namely, that personal guidance contains a miraculous element. Jim, Mr. Taylor, and a local member of the board, Dr. Howard E. Hansen, beloved minister of the First Presbyterian Church of Colorado Springs, went with the realtor, Gus Hill, to look over the site. As they approached the property, they were engulfed in dense cloud and unable to see anything. Even so, Mr. Taylor decided to offer the $20,000 asked by the owners. With no reason given, the money was turned down, and some weeks later the property was sold to someone else for the same figure.

I have repeatedly watched Jim's reaction in the face of such trials. It has been basically the same, expressing the outlook of a man fully surrendered to the will of God. In a recent letter concerning similar circumstances he said: "The manner in which they acted . . . would have seemed quite a rebuff except that I had committed it all to the Lord, and knew very well that I would not get anything there unless He made it possible in His own wonderful way." The "failure" of the Crystal Park project drew from Jim this unadorned, direct comment: "Circumstances proved that God had something else in mind." And this was evidently the case. Within a few months Gus Hill found another site for sale near Colorado Springs. Jim looked at it with him and later with Mr. Taylor, who enthusiastically bought it for $50,000 and leased it to Young Life.

That property was to become Star Ranch. During the following winter it became the new home of the national headquarters office, formerly located in Dallas, thus concentrating the basic Young Life organization in one place. This arrangement was maintained until 1961, when the growth of the work necessitated construction of a new office in Colorado Springs, at the cost of $134,500.

For some fourteen years Star Ranch was the nerve center of the Campaign. A group of businessmen from Denver and Colorado Springs, called the Star Ranch Committee, administered and furthered the camping program. By the end of the third summer the ranch was already being used beyond capacity. The overseers were convinced that it was wrong to turn away anyone, for they had seen God's blessing working in the lives of those who came. They located another camp, Chalk Cliff Lodge near Buena Vista, a hundred miles west of Colorado Springs, and in September 1949 recommended its purchase to the board. Shortly after the Star Ranch Committee had held a day of prayer for this project, Jim received a $25,000 grant from a new donor, a foundation which has since poured many thousands of dollars into Young Life. The new property was acquired at the cost of $56,000. The first camp to be held at "Star Lodge" (the name was later changed to Silver Cliff Ranch) took place during Christmas vacation of 1949.

It had been estimated that Silver Cliff would handle several years' expansion, but by the end of its first summer it was already crowded. There was an air of expectancy among the members of the Star Ranch Committee and the many Young Life leaders who had confidently turned their gaze to the Rocky Mountains. With the work evidently blessed as it was, God would not allow a promising harvest of teen-agers for Christ to go to waste. Surely the Lord would provide.

However the reader may feel about the events that followed, Young Life people, from Jim to the most inconspicuous volunteer leader, still speak of it in the same way as the British refer to Dunkirk. From beginning to end it was all "a miracle beyond belief." In the fall of 1950 Ted Benson mailed a clipping from the *New Yorker* to Orien Johnson, a member of the staff, which advertised an unnamed boys' camp in Colorado and specified "$250,000 will handle." It was sent as a joke. Ted had written on the card his willingness to go halves on the project with Orien, who put it on Jim's desk to share his amusement. But after one glance Jim knew it was no joke. Well acquainted with Colorado, he knew that at such a deposit price the property could only be Round-Up Lodge, one of the most famous camps in the Rockies, whose boundary began a mile away from the newly acquired Silver Cliff Ranch. In fact, Round-Up Lodge was right next door! Jim had spoken at Round-Up's closing banquet a few months earlier with no idea that it was coming up for sale. Quiet inquiry verified his guess and brought to light an actual price of $450,000.

Jim went to the board meeting in January 1951, afraid to mention the fabulous possibility at hand. He waited until the meeting was ready to adjourn before gathering courage to ask for five more minutes. Six lines in the board's minutes indicate the directors' approval of the project, provided Jim could raise the money from other sources than Young Life's regular donors.

As Jim likes to put it when he tells the story (and the present narrative follows his personal notes very closely), "two months and many miracles later" the bulk of the Round-Up property was purchased for $250,000, or half the original price! The total cost was met by eleven donors—the later default of one of them being made up by staff pledges to the 1956 fund drive. And so Round-Up Lodge became Young Life's Frontier Ranch. The story of God's dealing in all this was electrifying. People who heard of it stood aghast. When the staff first assembled at Frontier Ranch, they toured the grounds and held a prayer meeting of praise and dedication in every major building. It seemed as if Paul's testimony of "having nothing, and yet possessing all things" was somehow being experienced, in awe and wonder.

## The Young Life Institute

In the fall of that memorable year 1951 still another phase was added to the Young Life Campaign with the inception of the Young Life Institute, a venture in staff leadership training. The training envisaged was not primarily concerned with tactics and strategy in teen-age evangelization, though it ultimately proved helpful in that area also. Nor had the concept of a Bible school or even of a Young Life seminar played any essential role in the minds of the directors. Young Life has always believed that what is done for Christ should be done well. What accordingly matters is not *how* it should be done, in terms of technique (Jim abhors the word), but *by whom* it should be done, in terms of the quality of the Christian leader. With this in mind the curriculum was designed to develop mature awareness on the part of those who hope to guide young people intelligently. The intellectual and spiritual horizons of graduate students, it was hoped, would be broadened so that they might in the first place more effectively witness for Christ in our generation. The rewards of this unique training were originally conceived to be of mainly long-range benefit. The more staff leaders there were who, besides knowing the essentials of the Gospel, were grounded in theology, church history, Christian philosophy, adolescent psychology, and even the humanities, the more hope there was that the over-all ministry of Young Life could be wisely deepened and enlarged.

The original Young Life Institute recovered the tradition of the wandering scholars and mobile universities of the Middle Ages. From September 1951 to June 1952, the first class of seven students traveled to their professors, recapturing a medieval touch. Three major and several minor trips were undertaken. Needless to say, there was nothing medieval about the mode of travel. The "station-wagon grad school" went to Los Angeles, later to Chicago, Philadelphia, and New York, and finally west again to Portland and Seattle. Classes in Colorado Springs and Denver, plus field trips to small towns in Kansas and eastern Colorado under the direction of Orien Johnson, filled out the year. No classes were held in 1953.

The present Young Life Institute began in 1954 as a summer school at Star Ranch, with a class of twenty-five. At the time it was even planned to convert that ranch permanently into a campus. There were twenty-seven students in the class of the summer of 1955. In 1956, however, the Institute moved to the Fountain Valley School, fourteen miles south of Colorado Springs, where all available facilities are still being leased every summer. An independent preparatory school for boys, its 1,600-acre campus, with its Spanish architecture and a majestic view of the Rampart Range of the Rocky Mountains, has proved an ideal setting for the summer training of Christian leaders. Students testify that the day-by-day contact with Christian scholars who come to live there with them affects them as much as the subjects they master—emphasizing the truth that Christianity is caught as much as taught. Chartered by the State of Colorado, the Young Life Institute is empowered to grant a Master of Arts degree after three summers of study. The student body has doubled since 1954, when the Institute in its present form was first conducted at Star Ranch.

## Changing Staff Structure

This growing concern of Jim and the Board of Directors for staff leadership training had been motivated primarily by the rapid expansion of the Young Life Campaign. By the summer of 1952 the staff had already grown to 38 men and 18 women. As a result, an organization involving regional and area directors had to be initiated to provide supervision for the steadily increasing staff. Before 1952 every single member was directly responsible to Jim, but this was no longer practicable.

The Executive Director, appointed by the Board of Directors and responsible to it for the performance of the entire Young Life Campaign, would henceforth direct the regional directors and the administrative officers. His main task would be to communicate vision to both board and staff, to make the final decisions of accepting, assigning, transferring, or releasing the field staff personnel, and to develop high-level promotion of finances and public acceptance. To supply him with the necessary information on which many of his decisions must be made, he would have an advisory committee composed of the regional directors, the business manager, and the executive assistant, plus such other temporary members as might be deemed advisable. The executive assistant would be available for whatever tasks of an executive nature the Executive Director cared to assign him. This proved to be his main function, since the Executive Director was often absent in pursuit of his manifold duties.

The regional directors appointed by the Executive Director with the approval of the board would have full authority over the operation and development of the over-all work, finances, and public relations in their respective regions. They would provide close supervision and assistance to area directors, inspire and instruct the staff within their regions, represent each member of that staff on the advisory committee, and see to it that all policies were followed in their areas. There are at the time of this writing six regional directors, each appointed to a particular part of the country: Northwest, West, Southwest, Midwest, East, and Southeast.

The most important position in the Young Life Campaign has of course remained that of area director. It operates at the level of maximum opportunity for concentration on, and creativity in, actual service of Young Life. The area director can witness personally through direct contact with uncommitted high-school boys and girls. His main responsibility is to lead personally at least two Young Life Clubs, and he is also responsible for an effective follow-up program to help develop spiritual maturity in individual boys and girls who respond to his witness by making a commitment to Christ. Last but not least, one of his primary duties is to make effective use of the Young Life summer camp programs alike through proclamation, instruction, and strengthening of the faith. *Monday Morning,* a mimeographed weekly which first appeared in the fall of 1952, has been an effective link between headquarters and staff members in the field. It has recently taken on a new look under the editorship of Alec MacKenzie, the new executive assistant.

## Further Expansion

This rapid outline of the minimum organization forced upon Young Life by growing expansion and the resulting complexity of its work is not meant to suggest a relaxation on the part of Young Life leadership. Jim was still hard at it. In March 1952 a Seattle businessman flew him into British Columbia to show him an amazing site located in a setting of awesome beauty a hundred miles by water from Vancouver. It was so spectacularly scenic it had to be seen to be believed. The Malibu Club, at one time an exclusive yacht resort for wealthy Canadians and Americans, had been closed by its owner, Tom Hamilton of Los Angeles, because it failed to meet his high financial expectations. Neither at the time of his visit to Malibu nor some months later, when he first met Hamilton, did Jim seriously consider a purchase. The very idea was preposterous. Yet the idea grew, as the mushrooming camp program began to overflow the Colorado facilities, including even the newly acquired Frontier Ranch.

In December of 1953 Hamilton set a price of $300,000 on attractive terms, providing the deal could be settled that year for the sake of his tax advantages on a capital loss. The buildings alone had a replacement value of $425,000. The proposition was submitted to legal authorities and pronounced sound. Jim contacted the board's executive committee by phone, and the biggest transaction in Young Life history was consummated in a whirlwind of action. The first $150,000 installment was provided by four donors and the balance came from 1956 fund drive pledges. The Malibu camp operation began in the spring of 1954, and with it originated a new organization, Young Life in Canada, incorporated in Ottawa on June 7, 1954. Field work in the new country was begun in the West because of the important program at Malibu.

It is hard to realize the tremendous pressure involved in this breathtaking expansion of the Young Life Campaign. The purchase money for all Young Life facilities must be provided from special funds. No general contributions can be used for that purpose. The work involved in raising these funds is very great—yet ironically, the cost of all Young Life properties acquired to date, taken together, is less than it takes to build one jet plane. But the attention of Young Life leadership is not focused upon such comparisons. Instead it has been riveted upon the awesome fact that, although the total cost of all the facilities may have been only one-fourth of their appraised value, there was originally no human possibility of meeting it. The conviction that God has provided all along gives rise to a deep sense of responsibility for the use of his gifts.

In the fall after the opening of the Malibu camp the cumulative effect of many years of overcrowded schedule, complicated by overpowering migraine attacks, caught up with Jim. In October he missed a board meeting for the first time. Doctors ordered a prolonged relief from work and sent him on a three-month tour around the world. At its fall meeting in 1955 the board laid plans for Young Life's first national drive. After much preliminary work, the four-month drive realized an amount that freed the camps from debt and made possible many needed improvements. From the day of that great liberation to this time of writing the number of separate contributions has risen from 10,000 to 25,000 a year; the unrestricted contributions and those designated for support have gone up from $350,000 to more than $800,000; while the total number of camper weeks has climbed from 4,300 to more than 7,000. In addition, the Young Life staff today, as I mentioned in the Introduction, consists of more than 220 trained men and women, helped by many students, together with some 500 volunteer workers. To these should be added members of the various boards and committees who maintain the work of Young Life and extend it from headquarters to the various areas where the Campaign is active.

The Rev. J. B. Phillips, after completing his modern biblical translations, having lived in close contact with the Greek of the New Testament for over fourteen years, was filled with wonder and wistfulness. He felt as though the secret of human life lay hidden in those pages. Not as a mere theory or ideal, but as a supernatural, superhuman way of living. Behind the total narrative he had become aware of a Presence whose acts in the affairs of men filled him with ardor and excitement. Now that he had lost all incentive to appeal to proof texts he was met afresh by the uniqueness of the Figure emerging through the written page. He was forced to the conclusion that far above and beyond human experience, there is at work a Reality that can only be accounted for if the claims of the New Testament are true.

In a more modest way this experience of a candid New Testament translator has been mine as I have followed the unfolding of the Young Life saga. Once more New Testament Christianity has come into its own, in a small band of humble men and women sent into the Lord's vineyard.

# 3

## YOUNG LIFE ACTIVITIES AT CLOSE RANGE

*Recruiting for the Club*

NOW THAT WE HAVE SEEN Young Life in the founding, let us take a good look at what it has become. The pattern of its activities unrolls more or less as follows. A Young Life leader seeks out the teen-agers on the athletic field or at a school play. He befriends them over a coke at the corner drugstore. He spends all the hours it takes to break through a boy's reserve and win his confidence—and speaking of his new pal, Clark Jones, a colored boy, will exclaim, "He spends a lot of time with me, and I've gained a lot by that . . ."

How does a leader eventually get a young person to come to club? Actually, in all sorts of ways. It may be over a hamburger at the "joint," or an ice cream or pizza feed. It may be by the hint, "Come on over to Dick's house tonight. We've got an idea that might appeal to you." Or some amplified version, such as: "What about looking at a movie made at the Young Life snow camp last Christmas? It's going to be shown tonight at the club. Why don't you come in and get the scoop? It's fun, you know."

The club meets weekly, usually in the home of one of the boys or girls, whose parents then serve as host and hostess. The meeting lasts an hour. It consists of singing, comedy skits, and announcements of coming activities, and comes to a climax with a message from the Bible. This is presented in such a way as to capture the attention of the indifferent long enough for a thoughful look at the Savior. Evidence concerning Jesus Christ is examined so that any subsequent decision on the part of attending teen-agers may prove solid and meaningful. No undue pressure is ever exerted. The young person's right of individual evaluation is at all times respected. This practice goes a long way toward impressing upon the youngsters the fact of human dignity—the dignity of one originally created in God's image, however defaced this image may now be.

## A Club Meeting

When youngsters decide to come to club, the task remains to win them over. Various methods have been thrashed out over the years by the Young Life leadership as the best ways of giving them a sense of togetherness, once they have begun to trickle in. Some, as may be expected, will put in an appearance as a unit, with their "gang."

Young people are likely to feel at ease in a home, provided it is not artificially turned into a formal lecture room. And this is what is likely to happen if dear mother has her way. She naturally wants to make a good impression and have things look tidy. So the first thing she is likely to do is to line up chairs, only to be dismayed at the leader's saying that he'd rather not have it that way. The sitting room should wear its everyday, casual aspect, with chairs here and there and some furniture left in it, even if a sofa or end tables have to be moved out for the sake of space. Needless to say, there should be no greeters at the door, and formal introductions are ruled out. Let everything remain as informal as can be, to make the boys and girls feel at home.

The youngsters will be further in their element if activities start naturally from where they are and proceed at their level. Bill Starr,

Midwest regional leader, to whom I owe the specifications just laid down, puts the matter thus:

The kids are coming in from basketball, football, track practice. Some of them may be sweaty and grimy. They may be everything imaginable. Some of them may just have come from houses where they find a fight with Mom or Dad, or they may even have ducked out of the house because they weren't supposed to leave. You have every feeling imaginable in there. You must start where that kid is, where he's thinking at that particular moment.

This again is more easily said than done. Right now, the lad may be hiding under the piano, miles away in thought from what will prove the whole point of the meeting. Others and their gangs may still be talking over some business of their own. Not only should they all be kept happy, but they should be brought closer together with an eye on the purpose in view. *Esprit de corps* is needed; a group mind has to be brought about.

Singing will help at this juncture. There is nothing like singing, possibly combined with some kind of swing, to develop oneness in a crowd. Cheerleaders are well aware of this. But the Young Life worker should not follow his own preference and start with one of the great hymns of the Christain tradition. A funny old song—better still, a familiar chorus—will do the trick. Later they may pass on to something like the Battle Hymn of the Republic. By then, the boy under the piano may be crawling out, and be heard to say to a new pal, "Look at it there! Isn't it a kick?"

After they have sung for a while, and when the leader feels the group is with him, the minutes may be introduced. Rogers Carrington, Princeton area director, has pointed out that, following the club idea, in the early days minutes served the fairly normal purpose of relating, more or less humorously, what had taken place at the previous meeting. The element of humor has been preserved, and the names of those who usually attend club are still included, but the minutes are now pure entertainment, aimed at involving more youngsters. In general, they offer an opportunity for participation. Thus more barriers are broken down and some of the tensions relieved.

Whereupon there may be more singing. All the while, the leader will have done his best to get the group into a frame of mind ready to listen to what he has to say when the time comes.

The message will take the teen-agers as they are, where they are; just as of old the Master's message met people as and where they were. Before he proceeds, the leader will ask himself, "What is it that seems to matter most to these youngsters in their present situation?" This is crucial. The language used will also be that currently spoken by teen-agers. Through the years, Young Life has popularized a lingo along the lines of the kids' vernacular. Thus "Say, gang . . ." has become a normal Young Life expression in addressing a group of youngsters. So it is most likely to be used as an opening for the message.

The serious message in its garment of vernacular is well timed— never hurried; it is withheld until the teen-agers are ready for it. Several meetings may go by, in rare instances, before it is even mentioned. A staff worker learns how to practise the art of waiting, and this implies that of listening. What immediately concerns the youngsters provides the first point of contact in their own landscape of reality—the world seen through their eyes, that is, in the context of their teen-age tradition and their psychological and sociological setup. They come to feel more involved if their own idiom, with the slang it includes, is used as a means of communication.

When they seem ready, Gospel statements are introduced as possible answers to the youngsters' wondering about something or other. On such occasions, a leader identifies himself with his audience, mapping out the path along which he himself has been groping for light, and offering his own discoveries for what they may be worth. As he proceeds, he uses homely example and unconventional expression to make biblical characters live. Sooner or later a penetrating or devasting remark sinks home, and individuals become involved. The Gospel is presented to them in utter simplicity, so that they can grasp its elements, make them their own, and build them into their lives. Fine points and knotty problems of theology are avoided as far as possible—they are left to be dealt with by the churches which the young converts usually join.

There has also developed a general scheme for a convenient presentation of the basic concepts of the Gospel. I have repeatedly detected its main outline, listening to series of messages addressed to one week's "gang" after another at ranches. (Incidentally, the Western equivalent for "club" is likely to be used there—namely, "roundup" —to describe the time each day when youngsters and leaders get together for the club meeting.) Four basic themes are usually covered during a week at the summer ranch, or in a given period of time at the regular club: *Who* is Jesus Christ? *What* has he done for us? *Why?* What is the condition in me that caused Jesus to die for me? *How* may I personally make my own what his sacrifice on the Cross and his resurrection have accomplished?

Thus the New Testament message centers on the person of Jesus Christ, presented as the incarnation of the true manhood that God himself contemplates. Conversely, the awed teen-agers are led to realize that here is more than just man at his best, as we currently think of those we most admire.

Vital questions continue to be asked, with deepening sense, as the disclosure proceeds. Who, then, is the Christ? Why did he have to die? What did his sacrifice achieve, and what does it mean to me? How can I appropriate his benefits?

### Conversion

The club as a whole consists, in a perfectly friendly and open way, of boys and girls in all stages from frank paganism through recent conversion to Christian devotion of some depth and duration, including membership in the smaller "Campaigner" groups. The common ground of the club is simply wholesome fun and entertainment, including spontaneous discussion of teen-age concerns. The lack of pressure and the deference shown to individual belief and decision, (even at times when this is against religion), and the honesty with which they are expressed, have a large part in members' respect for the club, its leader, and each other.

A club member's profession for Christ or statement that he desires to be a Christian may be initiated during a meeting, but most likely after serious counseling with an adult leader. It is not encouraged to be dramatic and sudden. A sound and wholesome conversion (that is to say, forming a reliable basis for steady Christian development) is apt to be a slow process. No absolute rule can be laid down, however, for the conditions leading to glad acceptance of Christian life may have been developing in a young person for some time before he or she ever encounters the Young Life Club.

What actually takes place in the fellows' hearts and minds, no one knows. It happens in every different kind of way. One may have studied the elements of psychology and yet have to learn that Article 1 in any genuine knowledge of the adolescent is that there is not a single case that ever really duplicates another. Aristotle had an inkling of this truth in discussing such subjects as medicine and ethics. For him, ethics could not be a science because of the uniqueness of individual persons. It had to be called an art, like medicine, and be exercised accordingly. The same applies to any kind of practice derived from adolescent psychology.

Sin, whether visibly destructive or in its more silent forms of selfishness and lack of love for God and one's fellows, is fundamentally disloyalty. The task at hand is that of a transition from an inner setup of confusion and disloyalty to one of loyalty, or at least the beginning of that transition. A person—old or young—must be truly reclaimed; he must allow God to restore the defaced image within, for only in this manner can the new character, the Christlikeness, slowly force its way to the surface as the old self fades away. This means that tastes, breeding, practices of long standing must lose their grip on the soul. There is a word that appears three times in our Lord's parable of the vine in the Fourth Gospel (John 15:4): that word is *abide*. "*Abide* in me, and I in you. As the branch cannot bear fruit of itself, except it *abide* in the vine; no more can ye, except ye *abide* in me [emphasis supplied]." The word *abide* is the clue to Christian character. Loyalty to Christ must become what Plutarch called "a long-standing habit," if a convert is to recover his true nature.

A great deal of misunderstanding of the timing of a conversion arises when this slow subterranean process is not taken into consideration. Or at least the beginning of it, until the decisive move is made. After nearly thirty years of "monkeying around with the kids," as he puts it in his colorful language, Jim has become convinced that almost no adolescent is ever saved at the time he makes his public profession of faith. It is always either before or after that moment. A lot of them jump the gun, it would seem. When they first get interested they say, "Yes, boy, I want to be a Christian. How about it?" But the true hour of conversion comes later.

Some, on the other hand, may appear listless and say nothing, and then—ten minutes, two hours, or a few weeks or months later —who can tell?—they may go out to horse around with their friends at the malt shop. They get to talking and show up at the Young Life leader's home at midnight and ask him, "What's the scoop on this?" Jim confesses to having been surprised by boys he was sure were ready to close in, and they did not. Weeks, months, sometimes years later, in seemingly hopeless cases, some of them would come and say, "You remember that night you were telling about Joe Blow . . . ?" and so on and so forth. "Yes"—Jim would barely remember. Then the youngster would say, "You know, that's when I opened my heart." But was it? One of Jim's favorite sayings is that the Holy Spirit is good at follow-up work.

Thus the higher leadership of Young Life has been vindicated in its insistent warning that conversion should not be thought of in terms of its conspicuous aspects—that is, the more dramatic type of thing. Indeed, a sudden ostensible conversion crisis may be determined by circumstances which have little, if anything, to do with the intervention of the Holy Spirit in a life, a situation likely to result in a letdown, once the crisis is over—all in all, an exercise in futility. On the other hand, a gradual development implying continuous spiritual growth before and after the climax—if there is one —offers infinitely better guarantees of a genuine reorienting and regenerating of energies, as we shall see, for instance, in the lower East Side experiment in New York, described later.

Young Life leaders are realizing more and more that, wherever the crisis type of conversion is emphasized, a wider concern for the Kingdom of God may never truly come into its own. Hence, a genuine sense of life and purpose may be lost, together with that longing and preparation for the Kingdom which actually characterizes the orientation of Jesus' Gospel. Hearts are likely to turn cold and existence seem fruitless. A precious clue, this, to the kind of letdown occasionally observed in a converted youngster, once the "mountaintop experience" has ebbed away into some degree of disillusionment. Then a leader is left to identify, in the one concerned, that engulfing, willful self-centeredness which the Bible exposes as the very essence of sin.

## Patience and Prayer

Incidentally, an insidious difficulty awaits any Young Life leader whose Christian restraint borders on prudishness. A worker has to know how to let go, and when; the kids have a keen eye for that sort of thing. Mike Escalante only "went to town" in a North Carolina high school when his college friends began egging him on to play the bongo drums. After he had been playing for a while, two fellows asked him to join them in a number. He did, and the drum-playing along with his cutting up with them marked the beginning of a friendship between them, and through them with others.

A Young Life leader has to develop the faculty of rolling with the punches if he really expects to meet the teen-agers on their own terms. This means that they may have him on the floor and take him apart in a free-for-all. The treatment may prove hard to bear for one who is careful of his own dignity; but let him not worry about that. Experience has shown again and again that if a leader has it in him to stand apparent abuse, the kids will miraculously come to order the moment he indicates that the message is at hand. At Frontier Ranch I was once greatly taken aback to see Bob Mitchell make a fool of himself in skits as an entertainer, reaching truly professional quality in the act. He was greeted by a deafening, rowdy riot of laughter and whistling. When time for the message came, Mitch, as he is affectionately known, would lift his hand, flash a broad smile, and proceed. Amid a hushed silence the group would soon be confronted by the Christ.

Yet the worst mistake that could be made after initial contact and conversations with teen-agers would be to embark immediately on some topic of Christian instruction. One of the features that strikes the observer in this regard is the perseverance of a Young Life worker. I should characterize it as the patience of a cat, were it not that the Young Life kind of patience is eminently prayerful. Sandy Vitullo of San José, California speaks of spending hours and hours with girls, driving them to shop, walking all over town with them doing errands, taking them to games and to their weekly piano practice . . . Doug Kirk, now attached to Young Life in Victoria, British Columbia, tells of having closed in on a fellow, and subsequently on his thirteen-year-old sister, after repeatedly driving twenty traffic-cluttered miles and then tirelessly haunting the school grounds. At long last he reached into the home, where a whole family was befriended into accepting the Lord. All current Young Life practice—! William Mitchell of Denver, Colorado merely remarks in passing that a certain lad took two years of cultivation before he could be persuaded to attend the club.

Through all such proceedings, indeed, patience proves inseparable from prayer, a kind of prayer that does not attempt to hurry either God or man. "I have prayerfully tried to help them without being pushy," says Doug Kirk with reference to two backsliding Chinese girls involved in relationships with non-Christian boys. A young recruit on the staff, Sandy Hedlund of Seattle, Washington has already caught on. Whenever she finds her work disappointing, she is persuaded that the fault is not with the attitude of the girls nor the material she is working with, but with a lack of preparation and groundwork on her part.

We have gone so far astray in our prayerless Christian work in modern times that Young Life's insistence on patient, tireless prayer may well appear a novelty. These workers actually teach even pagans to pray, and this with the strangest results on occasion. Bob Barram of San Bernardino, California tells of thus having initiated into prayer life a seventeen-year-old lad who had just confessed that down to that day he had not even so much as *thought* of Jesus Christ. Surely here is an approach we seem to have lost sight of in this age. One can almost hear critics of Young Life expose it as belonging, among others, to the antiquated ways of the nineties! Think of it—a teen-ager proves a complete stranger to Christ, and instead of getting him into some kind of dialectical bull session, the leader proceeds to teach him to pray!

"Should I go about it like this?" the lad asked. Whereupon he began reeling out a prayer for the counselor's scrutiny. It was a good prayer—that is, all that could be expected at this point. So Bob told the boy to go ahead and tell Christ directly what he had just spoken as an exercise. Right then, all the finesse and polish went out the window as the kid began to pray a simple honest prayer to the Lord, on a level far deeper than the original improvisation.

## Counseling, Camps, and Campaigners

I have spoken of the wise timing used in presenting the Christian message. The counseling is also well timed and unhurried. It is at first limited for the most part to listening to questions. Young Life leaders shun the kind of early interruption that knows the answer before any more can be said. Listening patiently—and listening again, identifying himself with the kid's concern—the counselor waits for the moment when a real dialogue may be initiated.

The moment finally comes when the youngsters feel they can share their victories and defeats with someone who cares enough to listen and to help. Prejudices are erased. Communication is established. It soon becomes apparent that they have needed all along to discuss their most personal, most intimate difficulties with mature people but could not find anyone who would listen. "I just don't understand," is a confession they freely make as they look at the world the older generation is handing them. Obviously, neither parents nor teachers have been able to help them sufficiently in their uncertainties. And lo, contrary to current opinion, it appears that they do respect authority and crave to express what to them is the right kind of obedience. However, it takes an infinite amount of loving patience and forbearance to bring a teen-ager to the point where his defenses are down and he is ready to welcome the life-changing truth of God revealed in Jesus Christ.

All phases of Young Life activity thus emphasize the importance of question periods and free discussion. A current practice consists in the leader taking the part of the critic of New Testament Christianity and bringing forth the kind of objections heard in high-school and college groups. It is up to those in attendance to answer the objections. Whereupon mutual evaluation follows, the leader carefully avoiding any hint of a patronizing attitude.

Each Young Life meeting, whatever its nature, in one way or another invites further questioning of a more personal character and encourages private consultation with a counselor on a note of friendship·and mutual trust. "Cabin time" at camp finds its role at this juncture, though individual counseling may take place in many ways —by appointment, during personal encounter for other purposes, on the adolescent's impulse (even in the middle of the night), or regularly for a time in some cases. This freedom of the young person's initiative goes a long way toward creating trust.

"Cabin time" may develop into another question period, although the questions then asked are as a rule more personal. Quite a number of youngsters are more likely then to admit being involved. It helps to have a natural, accepted setting for private talk. What matters most, however, is the aftermath of cabin time, when individuals seek out the leader to press the issue into some kind of decision within themselves.

I vividly remember the case of a counselor, whose guest I was at the time, who on three successive evenings had talked to campers on sexual problems that came uppermost in their concerns just then. On the last evening, after the talk, cabin time was prolonged late into the night. A few campers then asked the counselor if he could come to their cabin early the following morning, which he readily agreed to do. It happened that his wife was ill and in need of extra care; also that I had to be driven to the airport in the morning. As he hurriedly returned home at breakfast time, a boy who had attended the evening meeting literally sprang out of a bush by the roadside and said, "Would you please come with me into the woods, and read the Bible and pray with me?" Which the counselor did, as if nothing else in the world were on his mind. Needless to say, he had no breakfast.

This great patience with shyness, slowness, obstacles of all kinds— and this utter devotion and self-giving that never counts the cost— these are what impress the kids. Yet I am sure that a Young Life worker, reading what I have just written, would insist that all I have said is merely peripheral, and that what ultimately matters in counseling is a complete reliance on the Holy Spirit.

The most important reason for Young Life's emphasis on weekend camps, snow parties, and summer ranches is that on all these occasions the leaders actually live with the young people and share their cabins. Opportunities for contact work and counseling then reach their maximum. Bob Brown has given a colorful account of such an experience when he took a station-wagon load of youngsters from a Southern California town to Malibu in Canada. He did not know any of them well when he started out, but traveling for three days quickly brought them all together. So much more so the prolonged camping experience and the journey back.

As things finally turned out, a boy he had noted at the outset for his aloofness, his shoddy character, and his profane language surrendered to the Lord and has since then continued to grow in the faith. Another whom he had also noticed at the outset, for his leadership qualities and friendliness, appeared to enjoy the meetings, but Bob could see he was not facing issues. Although a remarkably intelligent high-school student and incidentally president of the student body, he would not be honest with himself or with God. He admitted to his counselor that he was a "phony" and had been so for a long time. The moment came when he told several fellows that he had become a Christian, but it was not long before it appeared that he had been "phony" even in making his profession of faith. For two full years Bob followed him, only to see him slide further down. His dealings with these two boys in particular provided a perfect study in contrast.

This is the kind of happening and observation a camp experience can provide. Hard on the leader? To be sure. Tex Williams, area director in Indianapolis, commenting on a camp assignment which happily proved fruitful, candidly remarked that "any other benefit would not be worth the effort it takes."

It stands to reason that the work thus painstakingly done at the ranches is helpful to the clubs as well as to the Campaigner groups within them. These, as I have said earlier, are made up of youngsters who have accepted Christ, or—already being Christians—have decided to study, pray, and have fellowship together. Sometimes they are referred to as the "study groups." Their degree of dedication greatly affects the vitality of any club.

The state of mind of these dedicated young people lies somewhere along the path indicated above in describing the Young Life message, and conversion—at some point they have become involved, and now they want to know more about a message that definitely concerns them. They want to probe the New Testament; they need to pray. They are ready to proceed upon it in their eagerness to "do the truth." Like Bunyan's Pilgrim, they never miss an opportunity to ask their fellow converts how they came to this new blessed status of discipleship. This exchange of experiences and views in turn warms the heart of everyone, implying as it does a degree of confirmation in the faith.

Because this new fellowship proves such a blessing, Campaigners love retreats, especially in the mountains, where they enjoy the strange, sweeping, almost unearthly beauty of God's creation. They make themselves at home with this new horizon of reality. And when they return, in joyful commitment and unshakable confidence in the grace of the Lord, their very presence proves a transforming influence in the club.

The interchange between camp, campaigner, and club is well

brought out by Marcia Davis, of St. Paul, Minnesota. During her first year on the Young Life staff, she had in the club a loud, boisterous, unpopular high-school sophomore who used the Lord's name to punctuate her conversation, although obviously not in reverence. At a weekend camp the girl did realize her need. Gradually, as she studied the Bible with Marcia, then joined a Campaigner group, the Lord changed her life from self-centeredness to a genuine interest in others and in her God.

A further helpful element in the organization of Young Life appears in the work crews at the ranches and camps. These are for Christian development as well as labor. The only material compensation they receive is room and board. I have noticed that youngsters arriving in camp are greatly impressed by the fact that no salary is involved. "Hear that? Gee!" The sight of a fellow hard at work, yet flashing around broad smiles of friendliness and satisfaction, proves convincing.

## Boys and Girls

All Young Life Clubs are coeducational. Needless to say, sound personal relations are basic to the Young Life outlook, and awareness of practical problems helps to foster them. Leaders are well aware, for instance, that boys are concerned about the high cost of dating—indeed, of the whole ritual of movies, dances, meals, corsages, and other concessions to social pressure. The main problem of many a high-school student is the impossibility of having fun without spending money; financial issues loom large in an adolescent's world. So large, in fact, as often to build up a defensive resentment against girls, or "junky rock 'n' roll music," or even the over-all activities of other teens. Such a frustrated youngster welcomes the Young Life Club as a convenient haven where boy can meet girl in a wholesome atmosphere. Girls, on the other hand, know even by hearsay that Young Life circles constitute an auspicious environment for stable relations, sometimes leading to marriage.

The atmosphere of good will, fun, and a deep current of high ideals is contagious in both club and camp. The camps are particularly valuable for releasing tensions. A new spirit animates boys and girls on their way to camp; it begins to show the moment they board bus or train. It is not rare, at the Christmas season, to have a thousand youngsters leave home by buses, trains, and cars for locations in Colorado, California, Florida, and New York State. Although they may be drawn simply by the attraction of sports, sunshine, or good fun, this is a very natural time for the Gospel to have real impact on individual lives.

Most of the camps last a week—that is, long enough to make an enduring impression and launch the youngsters on new and vital paths. Memories are cherished for a long time. Perhaps, first, a barbecue party under the benevolent eye of Andy (Goldbrick!) Delaney, Young Life's favorite chef, will relax tensions and put everyone at ease. In all that happens the youngsters learn to be natural, to be their true selves. They "open up" in the midst of wholesome influences.

Healthy relationships are in the making once personality freely emerges and comes into its own. The masks of self-consciousness begin to come down and everyone has the cleanest sort of fun. Mountain boys from Cheyenne or Colorado Springs may make fun of young women still green at this or that new sport, but they mean well. Look at them teaching the flatlanders to ski! Or imagine a fashion show put on to advertise the cutest clothes and most picturesque outfits for camp. The show begins with a sing, or a swimming competition. Then boy and girl models file past amid hilarity.

Boys and girls trying to handle the sexual drives of adolescence find diversion from some of their anxieties once they are surrounded by the healthy atmosphere of club or camp. There is nothing like tobogganing, ice-skating, football in the snow or sand, to relieve overintense preoccupations. And it is a wonderful thing to share the difficulties of a hard climb in the mountains—to meet obstacles and prevail together, by friendliness, teamwork, and mutual help, while Young Life guides show themselves concerned for everyone's welfare and growth. Maturity is fostered in these shared experiences, which involve deeper meaning for both sexes, and prepare the young people to appreciate the teachings of the Master.

One of the lessons learned by Young Life leaders is that in a number of cases the key to wholesome relations between boys and girls is to be found in genuine, healthy friendship with members of their own sex. Unbridled sexual drives in adolescence often indicate the lack of such a relationship in a young person's life. Boys and girls crave the realization of a well-integrated personality of their own, and nothing can help them more in this than a trusted friend. Let boy meet girl—yes. But let boy meet boy and girl meet girl, too.

Here once more we come to the basic appeal of Young Life: the opportunity of genuine friendship implied in "friendship evangelism." Like all great achievements, friendship is an incarnation. It is note-worthy that the first step on the path to conversion in Young Life circles is the apprehension of Christ as a friend. Writes Susie Rear from Whittier, California, "I now have a friend that I can talk over my problems with and know that He will always understand and help me. The Lord has given me a reason to be living and a purpose to my life—something I never had until I became a Chistian." Who knows? Possibly one of the best ways to prepare oneself to understand Christianity is to cultivate the friendship of someone whom, in God's providence, we have met on the highroad of life.

# 4

# A NEW TESTAMENT PATTERN

*The Gospel of the Seeking God*

THIS, THEN, is how Christ's Gospel of a seeking God is being proclaimed to considerable numbers of adolescents in our day. By far the most impressive fact about the movement is that the features of it that emerge in boldest relief make up a New Testament pattern. The Campaign's way constitutes a new variation of Christ's "Go ye" command; nevertheless, it is one that spells the recovery of a unique feature of New Testament Christianity. If, as Young Life fervently believes, Christianity *is* Jesus Christ, then it must first and foremost be a *seeking* Christianity. "Someone cared enough to tell *me* about him," marveled a Young Life slum worker, originally led to Christ by the Campaign.

The great Jewish scholar, C. G. Montefiore, who first thought that there was nothing in Jesus' utterances that could not be paralleled in the Old Testament or in rabbinical literature, was ultimately arrested by the newness and high import of our Lord's proclamation of the living God as the *seeking* God. To deny the greatness and originality of this concept in Jesus' teaching, he confessed, is to beat one's head against a wall. In this unique element of Christianity the approach of Young Life to the adolescent is grounded. A more characteristic

49

feature could hardly be chosen to illustrate the fidelity of the movement to its New Testament prototype. Its significance as a clue to understanding the Campaign looms so large, in fact, that the next chapter will be devoted entirely to consideration of its working in actual circumstances.

The purpose in seeking out teen-agers, according to Article II of the Constitution of Young Life, is

. . . to promote an evangelistic Christian testimony among high school and college age young people by any and every means as God directs.

A. To introduce the Gospel of the Lord Jesus Christ to young people who are not personally committed to Him, particularly to the unchurched and the ex-churched.

B. To encourage, among young people who are personally committed to Christ, the development of a spiritual life which shall manifest itself in consistent Christian virtues and activities, including loyal and active participation within the organized Church.

The distinction between A and B makes clear another aspect of the New Testament pattern found in Young Life: namely, a separation of the proclaimed message of salvation, on the one hand, from the moral and spiritual instruction of those who have already accepted the message, on the other.

The New Testament distinguishes between *kerygma* and *didache*—that is: between (1) *the* event of all events, the coming of God's redemptive rule in Jesus Christ, the saving act whereby he has visited and redeemed his people; and (2) such edifying teaching as may be found, for example, in the First Epistle to the Corinthians.

This distinction is reflected in the programs devised by Young Life to further its work. The Young Life Club, already described, corresponds essentially to point A in the Constitution, or *kerygma* in the New Testament. The informal study group called "Campaigners," which forms a vital part of every club as soon as there are believing and dedicated Christians in it, is roughly comparable to point B in the Constitution, or *didache* in the New Testament. The close solidarity of the two phases nothwithstanding, the distinction found in the New Testament emerges clearly here.

An example of what has just been said may be found in the following paragraph from a report by Marilyn Horton, a sensitive Young Life worker in Greater Chicago.

My first year on staff I met a girl at ——— High who seemed fairly intelligent and well esteemed on the campus. The Lord laid her on my heart and I began praying that she would come to the club and spending time with her. She was a junior at the time and would not come to club. I offered her a scholarship to the ranch but she wouldn't go. Her senior year came and she still wouldn't come to club although we were good friends. Then in February of that year, after over a year of prayer and spending time with her, she finally came to club and signed up for a weekend camp. I was sure she wouldn't go, as she was the only senior signed up and captain of the cheerleaders, and they had two games that weekend. However, God wanted her there; she went, and the first night, after several hours of talking, she turned her life back to God through Christ. She moved soon to ——— and has been a fine testimony to the Lord through her college experience, a second divorce by her mother, and other trying circumstances. I thank God for the privilege of watching Him at work through the philosophy of Young Life: prayer, contact work, club ministry, a camp experience, and Campaigners.

## Young Life and the Church

If we may revert for a moment to the sections quoted from the Young Life Constitution, it should be noted that the message of salvation (*kerygma*) is to be addressed to "young people who are not personally committed to Him, particularly to the unchurched and the ex-churched." This explicit policy should set at rest the minds of churchmen who fear some kind of untimely interference with young people already involved in church life. As for the moral and spiritual instruction envisaged in Section B, the Constitution advocates "loyal and active participation within the organized Church" —a specification, one would think, satisfying to church authorities. Neither article is taken lightly by Young Life leaders.

The question here forced upon us is that of the relation of Young Life to the existing Church. The common referent in this connection can only be the New Testament pattern. The word for church, in both classical Greek and that of the New Testament, is *ekklesia*. Its meaning—the "called out" or "called forth"—expresses a gathering summoned by a herald. In New Testament Greek, "herald" is *keryx* and its reference is to the one who proclaims with authority the *kerygma*—that is, the tidings, the saving act of God in Christ. Thus the *ekklesia*, or gathering of those called forth, is of a most exceptional nature. The fact is confirmed by the New Testament writers' use of the definite article to make up the phrase "*the ekklesia*" of God or of the Lord—a phrase never found in classical writings, but consistently used in the New Testament. This is, for example, Paul's meaning in I Corinthians 1:2, when he addresses "the *ekklesia* of God which is at Corinth," meaning "the called out of God which *is* at Corinth." The appearance of the plural, the *ekklesias*, is equally noteworthy, for it applies to groups meeting in a house as well as to all the Christians of a metropolis. A perfect illustration of this twofold use appears in I Corinthians 16:19: "The *ekklesias* of Asia salute you. Aquila and Prisca salute you much in the Lord, with the *ekklesia* that is in their house." The implication is that the "part" constituted by a small body of Christians is one with the whole body of Christians. What is meant in both cases is the whole Christ, not just a fragment. This New Testament understanding of the Body of Christ should be kept in mind when the relation of Young Life to the Church comes under scrutiny.

Clearly, no section of organized Christianity can claim a monopoly on the Christ. The fifty-fifth canon of the Church of England is correct when it defines Christ's Holy Catholic Church as "the whole congregation of Christian people dispersed throughout the whole world." Yet a Young Life leader who holds an informal Campaigners' meeting with a group of professing Christians should be recognized as equally correct when he claims that they are a part of the Body of the indivisible Christ.

Earlier the remark was made that the application of the name "church" to a building used for public worship is foreign to the New Testament and constitutes a later development; further, that in actual New Testament practice Christians gathered together for edification and worship in private homes, as in Romans 16:5, I Corinthians 16:19, Colossians 4:15, Philemon 2. Here is still another precedent for Young Life Campaigners' meetings to be held in the homes of its participants.

Nothing makes for better understanding and co-operation than a clearly defined position. Presumptuous as the designation may sound offhand, we are at this point genuinely confronted by the *ekklesia* that is in the house of Bob or Bill or some other boy or girl—except of course for the fact that the sacraments are not administered there, and that the call of most of the leaders and members is not through ordination and confirmation. But the essentials are there: the Word is preached, and continuity with the historic Christian community is felt through constant and insistent reference to the Holy Spirit. There is no question that Young Life *is* a genuine expression of the Christian mission and thus of the Church. Freely granting that an expression is not an equivalent, it is only fair to acknowledge the Christian witness and achievement of the Campaign as that of a genuinely Christian movement.

## The Young Life Mission

As to its Church connections, Young Life is definitely nonsectarian. It is on the benevolence program of many local churches, but is not financed by any denominational office. Although its Board of Directors, the members of the local committees, and the leaders themselves represent a large number of denominations, they all work together as an organic unit, which claims an identity all its own. Finding its inspiration in I Corinthians 12—that is, as a member of Christ's Body —the Campaign has a definite ministry to see that no young person misses his appointed right to encounter a positive Christian witness and decide for himself whether or not to acknowledge the claims of Jesus Christ for his life. This task is so staggering in scope, and the need for it among our teen-agers so great, that Young Life chooses to leave involved doctrinal matters to the various churches, while concentrating its attention on the centrality of Christ in the Gospel.

How is this possible, some may ask? Does not the proclamation of the lordship of Christ immediately raise theological issues? Moreover, is not the Gospel record from beginning to end Christological? Probably the best answer to these objections lies in the belief that generated and sustained the expansion of New Testament Christianity. This was founded upon the finality of Jesus Christ, the Son of God and the only Lord and Savior. In his uniqueness he stood alone, meeting and satisfying the common need of which all the speculations and longing of men were the expression. He alone could say, "Fear not; I am the first and the last, and the living one." To be sure, there were moments when the heralds of the apostolic proclamation, in their eagerness to persuade, allowed their message to become freighted with confusing and obscure doctrinal refinements. Yet those who indulged in them were ever ready to withdraw to their base of operations and rest their case on the simple assertion that Jesus Christ is Lord. The wonder of early Christianity and its expansion is that it was originally entrusted, not to an intelligentsia endowed with great apologetic ability, nor to professional theologians, but to the rank and file of Christians whose witness was that of the man born blind: "One thing I know. I was blind. Now I see. Jesus opened my eyes." They were without a doubt extraordinarily effective missionaries.

This last remark is not an invitation to obscurantism. A Christian worker today obviously needs the kind of training that will allow him to communicate adequately with a highly sophisticated generation. Even so, a way has to be found to minister to teen-agers without bringing in issues—no matter how important—that confuse *the* issue, which for the Young Life leadership finds its summation in the centrality of Christ, in terms of who he is and what he has done. We have heard a great deal about the "hour of decision." It is time our attention was focused on the human *age* of decision: namely, adolescence. The minds of young people must not be confused. Let our teen-agers begin to see Jesus as he really is, and the Holy Spirit will take care of the follow-up with the help of the churches. When the Godlike simplicity of this issue is realized, a warm and friendly relationship is likely to develop between Young Life and the churches. Both pastor and the Campaign leader in charge will assert, like Paul, that "the eye cannot say to the hand, 'I have no need of you,' nor again the head to the feet, 'I have no need of you'" (I Cor. 12:21). And how can one lose sight of the fact that this apology of Christian co-operation in the twelfth chapter of First Corinthians leads into Paul's glorious celebration of Christian love in the thirteenth!

Young Life workers from every part of the field of operations agree that once teen-agers are won to Christ through the Campaign's ministry, they most naturally join a church, often taking with them their heretofore unbelieving parents. These same young people in all likelihood would never have darkened the door of a church had not Young Life sought them out.

## The Plight of Modern Adolescents

Millions of American high-school students today are not under any kind of Christian influence whatsoever. The most reliable figure according to Jim Rayburn, who checked it with the Federal Bureau of Investigation, exceeds nine million, or 75 per cent of all high-school youth. In addition, about 70 per cent of all youngsters who do attend Sunday school have stopped going to church by the age of twenty. Although great care has been taken throughout these pages to keep purely teen-age issues distinct from those of juvenile delinquency— which, incidentally, concern only 3 or 4 per cent of our youth—a few formal statistics suggest a relationship between the incidence of juvenile crime and lack of responsible religious training.

J. Edgar Hoover in his article, "The Sunday School—Key to Tomorrow," which appeared in the Sunday School Times on May 5, 1961, relates the experience of a juvenile judge who had had altogether some 8,000 delinquent youngsters under seventeen years of age brought before him for violating the law. Of these 8,000 only 42 attended Sunday school. Naturally, these and similar figures may not tell the whole story. On the one hand, quite a number of delinquent youngsters avoid being caught or are never brought before the courts;

on the other hand, law enforcement among juveniles has been intensified in recent years, so that what used to be looked upon as teen-age mischief is now treated as real delinquency. William Milliken, an amazingly efficient Young Life leader now working in the slums of New York, vehemently protests against what to his mind amounts to gratuitous name-calling. These are his words: "We have been conditioned by society (newspapers, magazines, etc.) to look down upon delinquents. Yet these learn early and fast once they hear about Jesus Christ. They are genuine because they have not been spoiled."

The relation to the churches and to Christ, the modern tendency to lump together all acute adolescent needs and behavior as "delinquent," and other related issues are handled with great care in Young Life circles, primarily because they pose a grave threat to Young Life by tempting it to depart from its New Testament pattern. The very kind of compromise with secular interests which has so greatly harmed foreign missions in our age also threatens Young Life. There are those who, with the best intentions, would readily support the Campaign for purely practical reasons. They point out, for instance, that it costs about $4,000 a year to keep one youngster in a state reformatory, or that the total amount of public money spent on delinquents may be estimated conservatively at more than $200 million annually, while a minute fraction of this financial outlay contributed to an organization like the Young Life Campaign will help to reduce the need. It would be hard to find a greater misunderstanding of the Campaign's mission. Young Life has never tried to gain acceptance in a community for the sake of the community problems it is likely to solve. The movement is not to be appropriated by any kind of general interest, nor treated as an arm of civic authority, nor domesticated within the framework of other institutions. Its chief concern is to safeguard its own identity for the sake of the integrity of its call.

This concern is not meant to imply a feeling of aloofness toward community, family, or even personal problems. None of the tensions that warp human life or add to the turmoil of our times find a Young Life leader indifferent. Like anyone else, he views the contemporary scene from his own vantage point, determined in his case by a constant awareness of the mission at hand, that of reaching adolescent lives for Christ. Secular issues are dealt with as they bear upon the accomplishment of that mission.

## Interpreting Adolescent Behavior

One of the unforeseen and unsought benefits of the Young Life New Testament outlook has been a liberation from the old-fashioned approach to the understanding of teen-agers, which assumed certain characteristics in a youngster's make-up, determined by a complex of external and internal pressures. More or less regardless of his own personality traits—and, I beg pemission to add, of his response or lack of response to the living God—an adolescent housed in overcrowded or dilapidated living quarters had accordingly been supposed to be headed for the street, there quite possibly to turn into a delinquent. When this happened, he was assumed to be acting "normally." This interpretation left unexplained the case of one who might conceivably react in what must then be called an "abnormal" way. Thrown back upon his own resources by adverse circumstances, he might find his way to the public library. With the help of a high I.Q., or a God-given friendship, he turns into a brilliant student—ultimately, in rare instances, into a genius or a saint. This kind of development, or lesser forms of it, occur not infrequently among young people from racial or economic ghettos, or broken homes, from which they are supposed to emerge insecure, maladjusted, and ripe for the devil. At the same time, statistics show that an impressive number of suburban, middle-class youngsters who have had everything pretty much their own way have yielded to the fascinations of the "beat generation." One cannot help feeling that an element in so many psychological miscalculations may have been the propensity on the part of proponents of the older approach for assuming that teen-agers feel, think, and act as adults might in their place.

But what is meant by the phrase "in their place"? If we were to put ourselves (as we actually are) into a teen-ager's place, surely we

would not react as he does. To put ourselves really in his place
we must become what he is, must substitute ourselves for him—we
must enter into his ways of feeling, thinking, and acting, and of
orienting himself to his world. If this is impossible for us, we should
at least record his behavior without prejudice or preconceived opin-
ions. Taking for granted, apparently, that the ways of thinking of
adolescents are identical with our adult own, quite a few psychologists
and sociologists—followed from afar by well-intentioned utopian
columnists who are instrumental in forming public opinion—have
condemned themselves *ipso facto* to overlook differences between
the teen-age mentality and that of the adult world, even where such
differences clearly exist.

The firm conviction of Young Life leaders, here at one with the
rising generation of social scientists, is not only that such differences
do exist, but that teen-agers live, and move, largely in a world of their
own. If communication is to be established with them, it has to be
in terms of that world, its tradition, and its vernacular. In their own
pragmatic way, and independently, these leaders have helped blaze
new trails in adolescent psychology. Their findings may well constitute
a contribution to the field.

## Significance in Brief

From the inquiry and discussion in this chapter a certain over-all
picture of the significance of the Young Life movement emerges:

The Campaign has found the secret of its identity and the nature
of its call in a fresh apprehension of the New Testament pattern.
At the service of a seeking Lord and the seeking God he has revealed,
Young Life has restored to full status the command of Jesus to his
disciples, "Go ye . . ."

The New Testament distinction between proclamation and subsequent instruction and strengthening of the faithful is reflected in the
programs devised by the Campaign to implement its mission. The
conception of Young Life Clubs and of Campaigners has been developed along the lines of the New Testament prototype.

The substance of the Young Life message derives directly from the apostolic proclamation. The policies of the movement are accordingly devised in full awareness of the ways in which this same proclamation has won acceptance in the secular order. Any estimate of the Campaign's position with regard to organized Christianity henceforth calls for reconsideration in the light of these facts. Far from being an organization antagonistically confronting the Church, or confronted by the Church, Young Life claims membership in the Body of the indivisible Christ. The Campaign's call has been to cooperate with other members of the Body of Christ in the context of chapters 12 and 13 of the first letter of Paul to the Corinthians.

Finally, one of the unforeseen and unsought benefits of the New Testament outlook thus revived by Young Life has been a real contribution in our approach to adolescent psychology.

# 5

# SEEKING OUT THE TEEN-AGERS

## First Steps

AT THE SERVICE of a seeking Lord who revealed a seeking God, Young Life searches out teen-age youth to reclaim it from the dejection of the far country. In spite of the note of cheerfulness that characterizes the Campaign's activities, the task has not been easy; as with every Christian task worthy of the name, it has implied the taking up of a cross. It may be illuminating to examine more closely what seeking out the unchurched teen-ager involves. Reminiscing about the early days of the Campaign, Jim makes this admission:

I went to Riverside High School in Fort Worth for most every single night, praying that I wouldn't get there. I couldn't stand it. It was horrible. It was an ordeal. I suffered . . . I wished that a big semi-truck and trailer job would come along and mow me off that highway. I couldn't stand it to go to those kids. They wouldn't shut up. They wouldn't listen. I couldn't even get the girls to get off the boys' laps. It's awfully hard to have a Gospel service with the girls sitting on the boys' laps. I couldn't get them to turn the record-player off when it was the lousiest music I ever heard. . . . For four straight weeks I never got to say a word about Jesus Christ or anything remotely resembling Jesus Christ. . . .

The new generation of Young Life leaders echoes Jim's testimony. Sandy Vitullo writes from California:

The girls were sort of snotty. . . , never warm. They downed everyone. We had a weekend camp in March. They went and had a miserable time. They did not eat the food, sat at meals looking sullen and nasty. They did not laugh at any of the entertainment (Mitch and Shelton) and had nothing to say about the meetings . . .

I have emphasized in the previous chapter the unprecedented and unparalleled character of the Gospel's disclosure of a seeking God, and also stressed the importance of the recovery by Young Life of the "Go ye" command. The question is now how this recovery actually takes place amid so many difficulties. How does a Young Life leader go about it in the light of experience?

Should one put this question to him, he would most likely want to have it rephrased, insisting that—whatever the method or procedure—the outcome is something that the Spirit brings about. No Young Life worker worth his salt will ever take credit for any kind of achievement. This all-important reservation should be kept in mind as we proceed to watch the movement in action.

A great deal of reconnoitering is needed before any positive first step is taken. Keen powers of observation will prove precious to a new Young Life worker, as will a good background in the social sciences and some familiarity with the latest literature on adolescent psychology. A proper introduction to school authorities is also a necessity, since the first step of the Young Life worker is simply to be seen around the campus, even if he does not say a word.

One of the best men now on the staff learned this lesson painfully while a volunteer leader in college. Jim Rayburn had been his club leader in one of the first clubs ever established in ———, and had been used by God to bring not only the youngster but also his entire family to a personal knowledge of Christ. Quite naturally, the young convert felt he should emulate Jim's example and let his life be used in a high-school situation at the first opportunity. This came during his junior year in college. A large high school near the college campus was to be his mission field. It was full of teen-agers who had never had a chance to experience a persuasive presentation of the Lord Jesus. They were a rough bunch.

The volunteer had somewhere acquired the idea that being a Young Life leader was easy; he thought it would be simple to start a club with these students, and went to the high-school campus almost every day to be seen and to get to know fellows on the athletic field or anywhere else he could meet them. Under the impression that things were going well, he did not realize that he was becoming an object of suspicion. He had not introduced himself to school authorities, nor was he always tactful in his approach and mannerisms. The weather was cold in the town, and he usually arrived on campus in a big black overcoat with the collar turned up. All these factors added up to a problem.

One afternoon the dean of men of his college called him in. The poor junior could see that he was quite irritated as he inquired, "What are you doing at ———— High School every day? I've just had a call from the school saying that you've been suspected and reported as a dope peddler and will be arrested if you ever set foot on that campus again." The school was closed to Young Life for years thereafter.

Thus the first step on a high-school campus—namely, to be seen and to hang around with the students—may prove a delicate one, especially if proper introductions have not been made and certain amenities observed.

### The Second Step—Key Personalities

The second level of contact is reached when the youngsters are engaged in conversation and a first informant is discovered. But what exactly is the leader's objective at this point? Suppose there are four thousand students in the high school concerned—is he to approach them one by one? The suggestion is preposterous. Then why this initial informal contact? Obviously, to find the key to wider contacts until the Young Life leader wins "the right to be heard"—to use a happy expression coined by John A. Mackay.

It is at this juncture that the social structure of a high-school student body must come in for close observation. Its organic solidarity is usually such that few students choose to remain by themselves. They associate with each other in particular groups, and the problem is to find the key that will unlock them. In the long run, this key may appear in the shape of an individual or of a closely knit core of personalities who happen to sway opinion strongly one way or another—key boys or girls, as they are called in Young Life circles. Win them over, and you will have access to the whole crowd they dominate. Admittedly, this procedure raises problems when applied to matters of evangelization. The instinct for imitation may start a chain reaction within a group, in which the experience of the majority has little, if anything, to do with genuine conversion. The same problem has been encountered by foreign missionaries, who have had to learn that to secure the favors of a tribal chief so as to gain access to his tribe is a method that may carry within it certain seeds of later hindrance or destruction.

When confronted by this and similar objections, Young Life leaders maintain that the influence they seek is merely such as will obtain an opportunity to present Christ, and nothing more. Even so, the danger remains; it constitutes the price a leader has to pay in order to penetrate an otherwise closed group. The best thing he can do to avoid it is to keep it constantly in mind. The fact remains, however, that in order to secure the right to be heard, key individuals must be sought out.

This is easier said than done, but patience and long-suffering are eventually rewarded. A good illustration is the experience of Norman Robbins, a Young Life worker from the West Coast and therefore a complete stranger to the East, who was sent to work in a large high school near Philadelphia. He tried to make friends with a few football players, but was completely ignored. In the course of his contact efforts he noticed that the four dirtiest-mouthed and loudest boys on the team had lockers next to each other. He tried to befriend them, but weeks and months went by without a glimmer of hope. Finally, all four started coming to the Young Life Club. One by one they professed the Savior. From this time on Norman spent much time with them, trying to develop their new-found faith in Christ.

The biggest lad among them had been in every tavern in town by the age of fifteen; wild living was natural to him. His close friend was almost as bad, but usually looked for his fun by getting into fights. Neither boy had ever thought of anything but football, graduating from high school if they made it, and getting a local job as all their cronies did. Norman helped them to enroll in a small Presbyterian college, where both made the honor roll. One made Little All American in football as well, and today is a fine Christian coach in a high school. He has even been elected president of his college alumni association. The other, after graduating, worked for several years on the Young Life staff and has become a leader in Christian education.

Norman lost contact with the third boy, although when last heard from he was still a professing Christian. The fourth boy later married a Christian girl from the club, and they have both worked for years in a suburban Baptist church where he is a deacon. Norman, now in his twentieth year with Young Life, did not tell me how these four boys by their example helped to reach others, but there is no doubt that they did.

On occasion, befriending a few key boys may start a stampede to join the club. After apparently futile efforts, Scott Oury, who had been on the Young Life staff for only two years, managed to make a contact that literally hit the jackpot. He had been doing a lot of contact work with members of the track and football teams at a big high school—had "run" a great deal with them and made quite a number of friends. Yet because of unfounded rumors that Young Life had political overtones, his club was averaging only twenty at a meeting. He decided to get together with four or five of the leaders and talk to them frankly about coming to club. He wanted them to see for themselves what was going on. If they liked what they saw, why should they not get their crowd to come? In short, he had to show them first of all that the Young Life Club was just what it purported to be.

He decided to seek out four key boys in the locker room just as school was over for the day, ask them to come to his car for a minute, and present his idea to them there. As he walked into the room he was immediately greeted by a couple of fellows he was not looking for, and noticed by several others. When he finally found the four he was after, the others overheard him say, "Come on outside for a minute—I want to talk to you," and instead of four following him out there were at least eight, which meant he could not possibly get them all into the car to talk. By this time the school day was over and a stream of youngsters was going past; before he could begin his "sell" the eight boys were inviting curious friends from the stream to join in, with remarks like, "Come on over, Joe—you need this!"

This illustrates the individual and unpredictable character of every personal contact and sequence of events leading to conversion, made up as they are of many trifling circumstances; and shows in a small way why the quality of the seeking person will always be the important thing rather than any fixed technique. In this instance, when Scott began to talk there were at least fourteen boys clustered around the car or leaning against it, and still more walking by. It was touch and go whether the crowd would respond to the idea of club or just mock it. Instead of three or four good friends, here he was talking to a crowd, including some he did not know and others who did not know him. However, they did know the four leaders. As he progressed in selling the idea of the club it became apparent that the response was positive, largely due to their presence. By the time he had finished they were talking excitedly about the ranches. The pressure was off. It was late in the year and some of the fellows could not attend club meetings because of their already full schedule of activities. But those who did go dispelled the false rumors, and when school opened in the fall a new life began for the club.

## Reaching the Individual

Once the leaders that students look up to for orientation have been won over, there is no limit to the Young Life worker's outreach. The most hardened youngsters are drawn in and are sooner or later bound to come face to face with the Christ and his claims on their life. Rex King, now area director in Nebraska, tells of a lad who was hard to meet, who associated with a tough group. He showed no interest whatsoever in the Young Life Club. Rex began praying that God would help him to get to know this boy, and for almost a year and a half he continued to try to befriend him and speak to him. Rex believed, as do all Young Life workers, that persevering prayer and long-suffering constitute the very core of the Young Life quest and outreach.

During the basketball season Rex invited part of the team to his home for supper, after which they decided to start a Bible study group. Because the "first string" came, the rebellious lad decided to come. He participated very little, but at least he would now speak to Rex. What was more encouraging was that he began coming to the club regularly. That summer he came with Rex to the Malibu ranch, where he listened most of the week. One night he admitted frankly that he did not want to become a Christian. Rex told him it was his right to decide. The next night the Young Life speaker talked about the Cross. Afterward Rex listened to the lad opening his heart to Christ.

The following year in school was his last. His coach could not get over the change that had taken place in him. His teachers were impressed by his reborn life. His former friends respected what they saw in him and found themselves put on their mettle by his example. His parents began going to church with him. The boy has now gone to college, where he is finishing his last year, and his example has proved so convincing that his own brother has recently become a Christian.

The classic poetic formulation of the way in which this young rebel was made captive to Christ would, of course, be Francis Thompson's *Hound of Heaven.* Whatever the reader's opinion of Young Life's use of key boys as on opening wedge to a large group, it must be clear throughout these pages that, in the last analysis, the Campaign's emphasis *is* on the individual person.

Another story is told by Brent Johnson, area director in Wichita, Kansas, who on a certain Christmas day spent an hour talking with a boy at———Prison Farm. The boy had been convicted of two car thefts and sentenced to six months; his parole had been revoked. His family was quite poor, and his brother was serving a two-year sentence for armed robbery. This young man whom the leader was befriending on Christmas day had attended the Young Life Club a few times, but Brent knew him only by reputation. His attitude was not affected by these discouraging facts. Here was an adolescent in distress, a lost sheep. Through the help of the assistant chief of police, the judge, and co-operative parents, he had him paroled to attend a winter ski camp and finish school in January.

It must have been a thrilling experience to help free this youngster to consider the opportunity for release from the bondage of self a merciful God had granted him. It was the lad's first exposure to the redeeming power of Christ. His response was positive, yet with little expression at first. After graduating from high school he worked as a shoe salesman while preparing to enter college. He recently brought two of his old drinking friends to Frontier Ranch at a time when Brent Johnson happened to be there. Deep was the latter's joy when he heard the young man pray in faltering language a simple yet meaningful prayer of commitment to Christ.

These abbreviated case studies should make it clear that, while Young Life has in a certain sense initiated new methods of approach to the evangelization of teen-agers, it cannot be said the secret of its effectiveness lies in its "techniques." There is no such thing as a Young Life technique. Jim Rayburn shuns the word and all the ready-made gimmicks it implies. As Roy Riviere has put it, the Young Life Campaign does not evangelize via a "program," or via "materials." Rather, it evangelizes via adult leadership. Roy puts the whole matter in a nutshell with the remark, "Interestingly enough, our critics point out as a weakness of our work that we are leader-centered. We shake our heads in some bafflement at this, because that's our greatest source of strength."

Every great work of art has always been an incarnation. The same is infinitely more true of Christian work worthy of the name. In seeking out teen-agers, a Young Life leader means to act in utter self-effacement. With the awe of wonder, he expectantly looks at what the Lord is going to do next.

Ken Wright, area director in St. Paul, likes to recall an experience that revolved around an unusual group of four boys he once met in a large California high school. They were outstanding leaders in every respect: in athletics, school government, social life, and also musically. They had formed a quartet which Ken first heard at a high-school assembly. As he listened, he prayed a silent prayer on their behalf that God would somehow break through and meet them.

A short time later Young Life had a weekend camp, and these boys signed up for it. They listened intently to the speakers throughout the week. The final noon camp ended with a suggestion to all who were interested to go back to their cabins, where they would find opportunity to talk with their club leaders and counselors. Ken was new to the work at the time and did not know whether anyone would show up—as if he doubted God's ability to reach young people.

He sat alone in the cabin for about five minutes. Then the door opened and fifteen youngsters, including the quartet, came in. He reminded them that they would have time later to pack and that this time was to be given to counseling. They said that they wanted to know how to become Christians. This Young Life leader could not believe what he heard, and went around the room asking each one specifically whether this was his personal intention or just a form of tagging along. Once he was convinced that they meant what they had said, he introduced them to the redeeming power of Christ.

What happened next may be said to represent the "key boy" process in reverse. Instead of uninterested high-school leaders being coaxed into joining, so that access could be gained to a larger body of students, here was an instance of an actual group of converts making quite an impression on the student body at large. The workings of God began to make headlines in the school. Kids started asking questions. How could they find what Dick and Ron and the other fellows had? Meanwhile the new converts met each week for Bible study and prayer. They grew in the Lord. Ken made it a point to meet each one personally. The freshness of their walk with Christ gave him great joy. Their problems henceforth were his problems; he had become genuinely involved with a group of youngsters who meant business with God.

He still prays for them. One of the boys, Ron, found his way to Princeton Theological Seminary to prepare for the ministry. And it should be noted that there are men in at least twenty seminaries in America today who were either won to Christ in the Young Life program, or stimulated in their faith to the point of studying for the professional ministry.

## Real Communication

The case studies thus far presented should not lull the reader into believing that, in spite of some undeniably rough spots, the going is easy for the Young Life leader who seeks out teen-agers for Christ. The confessions of Jim and of a younger leader on the opening pages of this chapter should warn us, if need be, against false optimism. Possibly at the root of the difficulties encountered is the obvious fact that adolescence is one of the most critical periods of life. A teen-ager is confronted by troublesome changes in his own body and personality. New demands are made upon him by his need for adjustment, his struggle to mature. His sexual appetites are awakened. He worries about what an adult would call little things—but such things as pimples on his face are not a small matter to an adolescent. Nor are problems pertaining to dating, necking, and petting. There is an anxiety to be accepted, a keen desire to be popular with everyone. He even wonders about the true nature of love. In the context of this wonder appear personal concerns about the selection of a career or a marriage partner. Religious issues lurk in the background of many of these unrelieved tensions. There is loneliness and an unexpressed, mostly unconscious need for qualified adult guidance. Finally, as uncertainty piles upon uncertainty there is boredom, a basic inability to concentrate on anything.

One of the first difficulties a Young Life leader faces when he comes to deal with individuals is to get a teen-ager to expose his true nature.

Bill Starr, a regional director for the Midwest, has come to the conclusion that by the time a young person is adolescent he is a master
at deception. In Bill's own words, "He knows how to be what he is
supposed to be around the people for whom he has some sort of
respect, and he knows exactly what he ought to be around the kids
that know him best, around his crowd. He is literally a split personality."

To seek out a teen-ager for Christ, therefore, means bringing him
to the place where he can take off the mask and bare his heart to
the Seeker. Once he can do this with the Young Life leader, it will
begin to happen with other people, too. He will be progressively
enabled to be genuine. As Ron Hanna of Tacoma, Washington has
correctly said, and as I have mentioned earlier, "a transfer of loyalty is
involved." This transfer, from the shallow loyalties to which a mask
is the only possible response, to a deeper and true loyalty, necessarily
implies a process of polarization. No wonder the process must be slow.

Not only should teen-agers not be treated alike, nor timetables be
set for their conversion. The truth goes deeper. It concerns the
danger already mentioned in connection with seeking out key boys:
namely, of what might be called bandwagon Christianity—thus an
objection temporarily silenced may reappear in a new form. A most
sensitive leader, Joyce Hamlin, whom I had the pleasure of meeting
at Frontier Ranch, has formulated a keen diagnosis of this danger.
She thinks of her dealings with teen-agers, not in terms of dramatic
incidents but in terms of moments when she became attuned to the
personality of another—when her inmost, genuine self quietly reached
out and made contact with a teen-age girl in depth, eliciting a
genuine response from the other person. In the light of this conviction, she feels that Young Life faces a real danger in trying to reach
youngsters *en masse* at the Colorado or Canadian ranches, through
huge clubs and large Campaigner groups. According to Joyce there is
danger in a bandwagon response to God. For, in truth, there is no
such thing. The only valid response to God is a wholly individual
matter, which involves the very soul of the teen-ager. There is need
for times of real honesty with teen-age girls, an honesty that is pain-

ful. It is easy enough to laugh and joke with them, but infinitely harder to face them as they are and confront them with themselves. Yet they need this and will appreciate it more than a surface friendship.

Obviously, this ever recurring problem of communication is a two-way affair. What Joyce suggested is that there are many ways in which a Young Life leader could give way to laziness. He may be satisfied with easy-going social contacts with teen-agers he finds congenial. But this will occur only in rare cases, for aside from the ardor of the staff, the faculty of candid self-criticism has become one of its main characteristics. I come across evidence of this on every side. Take the experience of Roy McKasson as counselor at the Malibu club. He was at the time a big college athlete. And whom did they assign to him but four small, nonathletic youngsters with whom he could not find any common ground—the fault being admittedly his own. He freely conceded his inadequacy, a true prerequisite to genuine Christian work. Instead of saying that each of the four lads came to know Christ in a personal way, Roy included himself and hailed "the work of the Spirit in all five of our lives."

One discovery a Young Life worker makes while seeking out teen-agers is that his quest will often move in a way that reflects his own nature. We only know that which we are. If a leader can make this admission he is likely to sharpen his self-criticism. He will then be ready to concede that the difficulties he encounters may be, at least in part, of his own making. For example, Joan Thompson, who works in the Greater Seattle area, has been led to take all the blame for the unpleasant things that have happened to her. She says, "I find that in most of the disappointing experiences I have had I have been disappointed in a selfish way, rather than that the kids have been way out of line." She relates her experience with a girl of closed mind if ever there was one. If Joan pressed her, this conceited teen-ager would admit that she was 98 per cent perfect and not 100. Joan got nowhere with her. To be sure, she was disappointed in the girl; but she is now chiefly disappointed in herself because, as she sees it, she tried to force her own ideas on her instead of accepting her as she was.

Joan adds with utter sincerity that she was doubtless also disappointed because she could not count another convert to her credit. This leader is eminently teachable, so the lesson was not lost on her.

Later, while counseling with a virtually impossible set of young women, she had one of her most rewarding experiences. Contrasting this instance with her previous failure with the conceited girl, she had this to say: "Maybe these two experiences were different because *I* was different." She had found a clue to the difficulties inherent in the personality of a leader. Yet once these difficulties have been acknowledged and the personality fault squarely faced, real outside difficulties may be more adequately traced to their source.

# 6

# ROADBLOCKS

## Relation to the Church

ALTHOUGH THE INTEREST of Young Life is ultimately focused on the individual, a constant effort is made from the beginning to reach as large a group as possible. And in order to expose the greatest available number of teen-agers to the living Christ, the movement was led to make the local club the center of its activities.

Among the most pressing issues for Young Life is that of its future relations with churches. I have already presented (see chapter 4) the respective positions of the parties involved, and this in the context of the most conclusive New Testament evidence. It has appeared that Young Life is by birth and by right an expression of what the New Testament calls the *ekklesia* of God, or of the Lord. Granting—as I have said earlier—that an "expression" is not an "equivalent," it is unthinkable that the Campaign's status should be put in jeopardy, or even be in any way questioned.

The trouble is, however, that too many churchmen have not as yet viewed the Campaign in this light. Not only do they fail to acknowledge Young Life as a genuine expression of the Christian mission, and thus of the Church, but they look upon it as if it were merely an ancillary organization meddling in Church affairs. Some even go so far as to question the relevance of a special evangelistic approach to teen-agers—glaring statistics to the contrary notwithstanding.

They assert, for example, that the situation at hand constitutes not so much a youth problem as a total problem. What reason then can there be for this total problem to be attacked at the adolescent level? Teen-agers cannot thus be singled out for consideration, they argue. We dare not lose sight of the complete picture, that of the world's need for the Savior. It may even be that churches have failed with adults more than they have with teen-agers; that the core of the difficulty actually lies in the Christless home, the home of the indifferent. Again, when it is claimed that the upper age bracket of Sunday school young people has suffered the greatest losses, is it not a fact that high-school graduates leave the community to go to college? If the whole truth were known, Church critics of Young Life conclude, it would appear that the teen-age church record is better than that of their parents. Should Young Life then pursue its independent course, it and not the youngsters would become the problem. Such, in substance, is the position of ministers who question the status of Young Life and the relevance of its ministry.

Whatever the merits of these and similar objections, the sad fact is that they are on occasion implemented by attitudes bordering on fanaticism. Stan Voth, a Young Life leader in Pennsylvania, once took a girl and one of her friends, both converted at Star Ranch, to the youth fellowship group of a local church. His motive for doing so was to promote the girls' interest in becoming a part of that church program—incidentally a current follow-up practice on the part of Young Life workers. In this particular instance, one of the ministers thought that Stan was attending the group to proselytize new members for Young Life—in other words, to steal teen-agers from that church! After enduring the clergyman's scathing denunciation for doing what he had thought was the right thing, Stan was left to ponder the ironic fact that the greatest opposition he had ever encountered in his work with Young Life was from one who claimed to serve the same Lord.

One of my former students, Dan Kamarnicki, now serving in

North Carolina, confessed to me that his greatest shock and discouragement came early in his ministry, when he became aware of the fact that practically all the opposition he was meeting as a Young Life worker came from religious leaders, both lay and clergy.

A depressing number of such testimonies have reached me in the course of my research. Yet no useful purpose could be served by dwelling on them. I shall limit myself to just one more illustration, which I owe to a dedicated and highly respected leader of Young Life whom we have already met in these pages: Bill Starr, regional director for the Midwest. His most distressing encounter occurred during his second year of service in one of the states of the Pacific coast. He was asked by the local executive secretary of the Council of Churches to report to his office. When he responded in the most courteous manner, the secretary bluntly asked him, "Why didn't you come to me for permission to do your work in this city?" Bill was shocked. He did not see how the purity of his motives could be questioned. Besides, he had suddenly been made to realize that here was one who thought of himself as czar of all Christian activities in the neighborhood.

Since then, Young Life has been better related to the Christian leadership in the entire area. Yet some kind of tension remains, and it seems to be the same everywhere in spite of the fact, noticed at every turn, that Young Life converts most naturally join a church once they come of age spiritually.

## Group Pressures

Contrary to some current sociological thinking, a large proportion of problem teen-agers come from overprivileged homes. These blasé youngsters who have everything their own way are often apt to add up to a dead weight, once they allow themselves to indulge in the membership of a Young Life Club or even Campaigner group.

Bud Bylsma, who works in San Jose, California, traces many of his difficulties to such seemingly lifeless members. He characterizes them as having no problems, as being well cared for at home and lacking any concern for Christian living, although they will often confess to a completely conventional faith. Ron Hanna, whom we have already met, knew his greatest disappointment in trying to reach a lad who came from a wealthy suburban family. The boy had fine Christian parents on whom his teen-age conflict with authority focused.

Wealth may prove a stumbling block because of its influence upon a young person's background, yet here again sociological prognostications may go awry. Charles Scott, area director in Jacksonville, Florida, told me about a boy whose mother had been married and divorced six times, and was currently single. During the successive marriages the boy had been taken along to many states and several foreign countries. His attitude bordered on the cynical. When the Young Life Club in his school proved a success, the lad, now an athlete and a born leader, began cautiously to attend. At first he was suspicious of any attempts at friendship, but he slowly warmed up toward the leader. A member of the local committee gave him a scholarship to one of the Colorado ranches, and he went, and found Christ there. He is now an assistant club leader.

Group pressures exert a tremendous influence on teen-agers, and this is rarely to the good as far as their spiritual life is concerned. Here Charles Scott, a keen observer, once more provides a story in illustration, about a lad who attended his club in ———, Tennessee. Charles was interested in him for two reasons: the boy was openly rebellious toward the message at club meetings, an unusual attitude in the South; and he was the leader of a sophisticated gang, many of whom came because of him—the key boy issue again. For two and a half years the Young Life leader prayed for the fellow. One day, at the boy's request, Charles talked with him for hours. He disclosed his fear of group pressures if he became a Christian. At one point he told the leader that he had accepted Christ. Shortly thereafter Scott had to be away for a month. When he returned, he called up his new "convert" to see what he was doing. The boy was at a fraternity rush and never returned the call. Later, when they met by accident, he had turned cold and indifferent. He was obviously caught in the mesh of hard-core group relationships.

The public at large does not realize the unbelievable degree of emotional tension to which many of our teen-agers are subject. Their mental agony and confusion is bound to affect, for better or worse, their reaction to the Young Life quest. Jack Carpenter, Connecticut staff representative, submits an instance of what he vividly calls "the products of a sick, materialistic, and complexly problematic society in the New York City commuter towns of Connecticut (Greenwich and Darien)." One of these products, whom Jack met as a junior in ————High, was so emotionally tense that he suffered from a bleeding ulcer, had to be operated, and had eight feet of his intestine removed. He was plagued by psychosomatic problems at least partially due to family blow-ups and academic difficulties; also troubled by problems in youthful romance. All these factors added up to a deep restlessness in his Christless life. Hours of identification with his sufferings and long periods of guidance on the part of the leader finally led the lad to Christ. From then on, it has been both thrilling and rewarding to watch God at work in him. Discipline and maturity are now forming in his life.

## Adult Attitudes

The Young Life Connecticut representative proceeds from this example to draw attention to the ways in which success-mad parents and other community leaders distort and actually discourage personal commitment, both before and after it is made. He quotes a father as saying, "One hour of religion is enough for my boy."

"The warnings are up on all sides," this staff member says poignantly. "Don't let Christ ruin your chances of making yourself a success and being happy! Don't commit yourself, and you'll stay out of trouble!" Only God can break through this attitude, he concludes.

Even when parents make their influence felt in the right direction, their motives are often not the highest. Yet God may use them. There is for instance the case cited by Bud Bylsma of a high school in Maryland where the core of the newly started Young Life Club was a group of football players. These were the wildest kids in the school. Among the ruffians, and by far the worst of them, was a real ringleader. On the first night of club he was elected president, only to laugh it off and swear he would never come back. Once at home, however, his mother strongly urged him to return, since he was president. So he did—and ringleader he proved to be. Under his regime the gang made it a point to sing all the wrong tunes during services, did everything they could to ridicule and disrupt the activities of the club. In school, the disruption caused by these young men was so bad that eventually the football coach resigned. Yet the time came when, out of a clear sky, the rowdy ringleader professed Christ. So formidable was his authority as a leader that ridicule around him did not persist long, as he went around carrying his Bible. He graduated from high school and went on to junior college in New Mexico to prepare for entrance to the Air Force Academy.

He had not been in college long when an alcoholic father at home caused such grief and created so many problems that the young convert felt he had to leave school to help his mother. In spite of the difficult home situation, he grew into a beautifully mature Christian. One night, about a year and a half after his surrender to Christ, he was killed in an automobile accident. His New Testament was found in his pocket. The mile-long procession of cars at his funeral was a tribute to the influence he had exerted. With him in the car were three other boys, not seriously injured, none of whom were Christian. Two had been officers in the same Young Life Club. The next summer one became a Christian as a direct result of the boy's changed life and the impact of his death. Two weeks before he died he had told his Young Life leader that he thought he should go into the ministry; and his last witness in public was at a dinner at which he told about 250 adults that the greatest thing his mother had ever done for him was to make him go back to the club the second time.

One would expect adults to reveal the greatest concern for teenagers and to give at least a chance to representatives of an organization such as Young Life. Jack Carpenter's testimony, above, has already shown that adult concern, when manifest, is too often materially motivated and thus inimical to any form of spiritual commitment. To questions such as: What do we most cherish nowadays? What are our basic values?—the average American adult is likely to give confused and bewildered answers, unless the approach be at a fairly low external level. The views current in our midst today lack those qualities of vitality and dignity that would make a higher commitment seem worth while. For many of our contemporaries the thing to do in any kind of emergency, including even the cultural and spiritual crisis of our time, is to keep one's shirt on, to remain cool. Lack of overt enthusiasm is not far from being regarded one of an adult's best virtues. "You want to be an athlete, boy? Good for you. Make a name for yourself. Let no emotionalism turn you into a sissy and spoil it all!" This, I am sorry to say, is the kind of advice to which our kids are exposed again and again.

A Young Life worker I shall not name has confided to me that his biggest discouragement is the misunderstanding on the part of adults as to what Young Life is attempting to do and actually doing. He was thinking at the moment mostly of the coaches at one of the schools where he operates. His complaint was that last year they told the boys not to come to Young Life because its activities would interfere with their athletic careers. Most of these fellows had been coming to club, but now they have stopped. A club that had counted over a hundred attending is now running in the thirties. As another Young Life leader, Roger Harlan, puts it: what really hurts is the misunderstanding of those who seem to be in a position to understand—but don't.

"Be done with the indictment of teen-agers! The trouble is with adults." Such is the substance of an impressive number of testimonies given by Young Life workers. Exclaims Jim Rayburn about teen-agers (but then, he is terribly prejudiced when young people are in any way maligned):

They are the most open-minded bunch of folks in the whole world. That's one wonderful thing about them. They haven't taken on one of the disagreeable traits of adulthood as yet. They are perfectly frank about the fact that they are sinners. They buy that summation in *Romans* 3, just like that. You talk to them about "Your mouth is full of cursing and bitterness," and some big guy is almost sure to come and say, "How come you picked on me tonight?" And they mean it. "Sure, my mouth is full of cursing and bitterness. How did someone writing 2,000 years ago know that?" It makes a whale of a lot of sense to them.

This testimony is endorsed by a man who used to be a very indifferent member of Jim's own first club in Fort Worth, Texas, years ago. He has since graduated from Whitworth College, Spokane, Washington, and is today one of the outstanding leaders of Young Life in Canada—Bob Page. Here is one who has observed Young Life from all angles and must have a clear and comprehensive perspective on its field of activities. His characterization of teen-agers is incisive: "They disappoint me only in a very temporary way. They thrill me in a permanent way." But his indictment of adults, even Christian lay adults, is direct:

My greatest disappointment stems from a condition which seems rather permanent among Christian lay adults. It is one of apathy. There is apathy about personal discipline, about their neighbors and business associates knowing Christ, about putting themselves out to make a young person feel part of the Church; tremendous apathy when it comes to financial sacrifice to see a kid sent to camp, a staff member's family pay their rent, or to feed an orphan in Korea.

There seems to be very little interest in the kind of discipleship evident in the New Testament. I am afraid this is an abiding disappointment which makes others fade into insignificance. That there are hundreds of thousands who could know Christ but for apathetic Christians, is a blight on North American Christendom. I do hope that we can rear a whole mass of young Christians who are willing to pay the price for usefulness in the Kingdom.

What a realm of possibilities this last sentence opens up, projecting into the next generations, as it does, the work Young Life is doing today!

## Adolescent Instability

Should we then simply endorse what men like Jim Rayburn and Bob Page affirm, and conclude that the spiritual mortality rate among converts need not trouble Young Life workers? Most of the answers I have obtained to this question tend to show that while teen-agers, as far as their make-up is concerned, may not raise *lasting* problems, they do raise serious ones. Apathy is not an adult monopoly. Looking back upon his experience in Vancouver, the state of Washington, and Oklahoma City, Chet Starr, Seattle area leader, testifies to having to contend all along not so much with rejection as with indifference, even among teen-agers into whose lives he had poured the best of himself.

However, one is left to wonder whether Chet might not revise his diagnosis fifteen or twenty years from now, should he meet these same kids as adults. Some of the older leaders, and especially Jim, would think so. Thomas Bade, area director in Los Angeles, who has served for eleven years on the staff, is most candid on the subject. Says he, "The American teen-ager is a very unstable commodity. The same boy can be rewarding, disappointing, and rewarding again within the span of three days." Professional psychologists would agree. Instability is a basic element of the teens; so is boredom. And the two go hand in hand.

Only through a genuine contact with Christ can the teen-ager set his roots firmly and begin to show progress in maturity. To consider the instability of adolescence, therefore, as an obstacle in the way of evangelization is to put the cart before the horse. Judith Outerbridge, who works for Young Life in Canada, tells of inviting two girls to her apartment for dinner. She believes in dealing with teen-agers individually or, at most, in small groups. During the conversation one of the girls declared that she finally understood what it meant to have a "realistic" faith. "I know now that the Christian life is not easy. It is not based on how one feels, but on an active participation of the individual with Christ." The girl went on to say that she was experiencing in her daily life a stability she had not known before. Her faith enabled her to face life realistically.

A serious problem Christian groups everywhere have to face is that of false conversion. With Jim Rayburn at the helm of Young Life it would seem unnecessary to bring up the subject; yet quite a few

Young Life leaders express concern about it. Tom Gustafson, who works in Texas, cites the case of a girl, a student leader, who went to Malibu, accepted Christ, and came back to set things going in her school. For a year she seemed to be growing in knowledge and devotion and was most helpful at club. But in less than a year following graduation, while in college, she began to ridicule her faith; she got into personal difficulty, had to get married, and might have named a dozen boys as possible father. She has had one divorce and is still getting into trouble at every turn. Incidentally, here arises the issue of college follow-up which Young Life is now beginning to tackle in earnest.

Bill Starr has already warned us that the adolescent is a master at deception. The fact becomes a natural roadblock across the path of Young Life. It is curious that deception seems more noticeable among teen-agers with a rigid Christian background than among young pagans. Judith Outerbridge speaks of a girl she knows who belongs to a conventional denomination and who claims to know all the answers. Her life is empty because she cannot be honest; she is bound up by fear. In this condition nothing seems to get through to her. She retreats from any direct approach and denies all evidence that would embarrass her version of things. To Judith all this is but the symptom of a deeper problem—a desperate escape from reality and responsibility. A façade of piety once used in this way as a cover-up is likely to become an impenetrable wall.

Closely related to this type of make-believe mentality is that of the calculating youngster who puts on an act so as to be able to enjoy the fun that a Young Life program offers. Jo Davis, who now works in Tennessee, recalls a group of eastern girls who were assigned to her during her first counseling appointment at a ranch. They were obviously there to have a good time. They had a praiseworthy attitude toward the camp and its program and seemed to enjoy it. But at "cabin time"—that is, when counseling was beginning in earnest—they withdrew into their shell. It was like pulling eyeteeth to get them to talk. In their own words, they did not want to "get emotional." Usually they dropped off to sleep. A disheartening experience this proved to be; yet six weeks later the young coun-selor heard from one of them. During the past several years she had felt something was missing in her life. In Colorado she had been disappointed because she was still confused and unsure of herself, and hesitated to talk in the cabin, but now that she had been able to organize her thoughts she felt ashamed. Becoming a Christian had done wonders for her. It had taken her a long while to realize that something had happened to her.

All things are possible to God. And we have all heard that where there is life there is hope. But the reverse is also true: while death is not the end of everything, it at least marks an end to earthly waver-ing. It is the perpetually recurrent wavering that weighs down the most dedicated Young Life leader, especially when it follows after solemn professions of faith. Nothing is so painful as the heartbreak of the good and faithful servant. If only this ugly "thing" were not found crouching at the door again and again! But backsliding is one of the crises a Young Life worker has to cope with—although the word it-self is taboo in Campaign circles, the reason being that, just as con-verts are not to be counted, so a human being should never be given up for lost. Jim Rayburn recently put the matter to me: "Some of the greatest Christians who have come out of Young Life did several years of what you call 'backsliding,' but they could not stand it." Yet I take it that, all the while, some Young Life leader or other felt the hurt.

George Sheffer, Southwest regional director, permitted me an insight into the kind of experience that touches the very soul of a dedicated Christian worker, when he shared with me one such case of blighted hope. A teen-ager who had been entrusted to him when he was manager of Frontier Ranch had matured amazingly during the month spent there. On returning to the city he seemed to do pretty well for a while. Then he took to drinking. One day he asked if he could talk to his adviser. As the interview began in George's office, the lad made it bluntly plain that he had not come to be preached at. George agreed to limit himself to answering the boy's questions. For a year thereafter, the young fellow put in only a few appearances. Sometimes George would not see him for three months, although he made appointments regularly. Then one day as they were sitting together in the office, the young man blurted out this statement: "I've been out of high school around seven years; I'm twenty-five now; my life is ruined and entirely useless. George, I have only one ambition, and that is to die and go to be with the Lord."

Subsequently, George tried in every way he knew to help this fellow, but the lad proved undependable in the extreme. He would start drinking, hop a freight and go to California, get a job for a few days, buy some more liquor, and hop a freight for Seattle. This was the way he lived for seven years. George did all in his power to reach this young man, but got nowhere. Friends tried to help—in vain. The fellow recently called up, made an appointment for the next day, and did not show up. George does not know where he was then, or where he is now.

This good man insists that he has never forgotten for one moment that with God all things are possible. His dilemma lies in the fact that, though he does not know what step to take, he finds it difficult to give up. He has worked with the most apparently hopeless cases and seen God's grace established in the lives of those who truly gave themselves to Christ and relied on his power. Some of these men have now become outstanding leaders in their own communities. They were human wrecks when they came to camp. Because of such accomplished miracles, a man of God is bound to suffer—in the most tantalizing way—when confronted by a seemingly hopeless case.

To pursue the subject of instability along still another angle, Christian workers have to come to terms with the dynamics of behavior and the realities of mental illness. It is indeed highly desirable for a Young Life leader to learn what the science of psychiatry has to offer in dealing with unstable people. It is still more imperative that he acknowledge his own limitations. He must know when the time has come to seek professional help in order to identify abnormal symptoms and deal with them adequately. I am sure that George's case, related above, is a good example. I am also quite willing to believe that, on occasion, the will of God for a man in need can be mediated by the medical profession.

Men of George's caliber would agree to this last proposition, yet also insist—and rightly so—that recourse to psychiatric help may be overdone nowadays, even in Christian circles. There *is* such a thing as human nature in the raw. The plain fact is that this book about Christ we call the Bible is concerned from beginning to end with the redemption of that very nature. Mal McSwain, who works in North Carolina, concentrated his efforts for six months on a group of teen-agers who were, in his own words, "rough, vulgar, wild." They had been helped to some extent by coming to club and talking with the Young Life leader. Two of them had invited Christ into their hearts during a Christmas camp, but as soon as they returned home reverted to the same old gang activities. For a time they seemed to want to come back to Young Life. Then it happened! One Monday the leader found that these fellows had got drunk and with their buddies had staged a gang fight and ruined cars, lawns, and almost a whole house. The mystery of evil we have always with us.

## Boy-and-Girl Relationships

There are other, more subtle obstacles in the path of Young Life which must be avoided. For a club to do really well it must have a reasonable ratio of boys and girls attending. Tom Railey, Northwest regional director, has drawn my attention to this. He inherited a club which had a healthy total membership (fifty to seventy-five), but a very poor ratio of boys to girls. The first night he met with the club there were only three boys present and probably fifty girls. This had been the general pattern for some time. Contact work helped in rounding up more fellows, who would come once but be so impressed by the lack of balance that they would not come back. They seemed to decide that it was a girls' club, and they were not going to be the guinea pigs for it! A summer in Malibu helped to recruit a set of youngsters who knew practically nothing about Young Life. Through the grace of God they sparked a revitalization of the club, and before long the boys exceeded the girls in number. The picture is now the most encouraging Tom could hope for.

At a different and more serious level, on the other hand, a seasoned Young Life leader will have discovered that some crises occur in which boy-and-girl relationships interfere with the spiritual growth of youngsters. These crises go deep, and they are widespread. I shall limit myself to a few instances which throw some light on the activities of Young Life in this regard.

There can be a complete change of orientation, and ultimately of character and destiny, for teen-agers who yield to sexual temptation. Bruce Sundberg, area director in Rockford, Illinois presents the case of a girl who was a popular cheerleader in high school. She put her trust in the Lord the summer following graduation, then in the fall went off to college, got involved with a boy, and had to be married. Yet she pretended that everything was fine. She has now changed into a socialite whose main motivation seems to be to climb the proverbial ladder.

Imitation often aggravates this kind of situation. William Mitchell, Young Life area director in Denver, Colorado, gives the example of a most promising Christian boy who became involved with a girl and had to marry her. His equally brilliant younger brother, who had grown in the faith in spite of real handicaps, finally did the same thing, with the same result. In both cases there was a marked deviation from original plans. All were pursuing lives sharp and keen for Jesus Christ, until the crisis upset everything.

Anne Cheairs, of the San Francisco Bay area of Young Life, has seen this happen more than once. She particularly remembers a sixteen-year-old girl who went to Star Ranch and there made a commitment to the Lord. There followed a happy and strengthened life and conversation in and around the Young Life Club. Eventually her boy friend, realizing that her new interest in the things of God came between them, got her drunk at a beach party and made her pregnant. Lacking courage to break the news to Anne, she sent her best friend with the message. She has not had anything to do with Young Life since.

The problem of adolescent sex relations continues to concern many parents and youth workers throughout America today. The very fact that Young Life is keenly aware of the difficulties and has met them creatively within its own sphere suggests our need for these or similar modes of approach—beginning with our need for Young Life itself. Its leaders know that the problem cannot be disposed of in simple terms of rigid "right" and "wrong." The question as to what is right and what is wrong is one of the first a teen-ager asks. Most of the time his inquiry is perfectly candid. He just does not know the answer; he is groping for one. His natural urges crave satisfaction —to what extent should they be satisfied?

The paraphernalia of civilization—movies, radio, TV, books, magazines, newspapers, advertisements—expose the readiness of a good many adults to do as they please in this matter. Traditional standards seem to be denied by the evidence our culture supplies. What right do adults have, then, says a youngster to himself, to force arbitrary limitations on the younger generation? This much is sure: mere moralistic pronouncements will be seen as arbitrary encroachment and accordingly ignored. Ignored, that is, unless the older person, man or woman, forces respect by the quality of his own character—and unless his motivation is apprehended as born of undeniable friendly interest. The first point of contact between the youngster and the Young Life leader appears right there. A genuinely friendly approach on the part of someone a teen-ager has learned to love and admire marks the first step toward a solution.

To accuse Young Life of indifference in the matter of sex because of its refusal to be rigid and authoritarian, and because of its patient concern for the "readiness" of the "delinquent," would be to miss the whole point. The Bible reader knows a phrase, "the fullness of time"; divine teaching, according to Scripture, is grounded in that notion. Only with this kind of patience can healing and wholesomeness—that is to say, wholeness—come, if they have been lost sight of. So far as the security and guidance of teen-agers is concerned, Young Life with its alert, sensitive leaders, healthy program, and high standards contrasts sharply with the random associations of most high-school young people.

Moreover, there is clear evidence from counseling that the prospect of finding a husband proves infinitely more attractive to young women than that of illicit sex relations. Furtive intercourse, under a sense of guilt and fear, often turns out to have been disappointing to a girl. The admission is frequent: "I got nothing out of it"—though this may occasionally hide an effort to minimize the gravity of the transgression. Boys, as a rule more positive in their evaluation, are sometimes found to be so for the sake of boasting of their masculine powers, in spite of hidden frustration. In general, adolescent experiment in sexual matters gives rise to self-analysis and self-criticism amounting to disappointment or even disgust, and this opens the door for guidance from the Young Life counselor.

Along with the high personal morale of the clubs, happy marriages among Young Life leaders help provide a living illustration of healthful relations between the sexes. A similar personal tone is conveyed when a former Young Life convert brings his girl to club in a strong desire to share the Good News that changed his life when he was a high-school student, and the two of them then devote their energies to Young Life in various club and camp situations. Nothing impresses high-school students more than such living examples of happiness. When the adult world in general is able to offer such a picture, it will have done much to eliminate adolescent confusion about sex and marriage.

Once teen-agers have made a meaningful profession of faith, the sexual problem loses its sting. I have had opportunity to observe Campaigners and members of work crews at close range and to talk to them repeatedly, and they have on all occasions impressed me as people who had come to terms with the drives of adolescence. As Carol Zitz of Elmhurst, Illinois puts it, "Work crew was so much easier with Christ helping me. I know that I (and anyone else) can do anything through the strength of Jesus Christ . . ."—truly a keynote profession, which echoes Young Life teaching at its best. This deep and joyous conviction is not lost on other club members.

Jim Rayburn, in his column "Say Gang" in the Campaign's magazine, handles the teen-ager's situation in his typically pointed way:

First, *do not neglect the simple, more or less routine things of the Christian life*—Bible reading, prayer, church activity, fellowship with Christians. Almost every time a young person begins to feel cold and unproductive in his Christian life it is because he is sadly neglecting these things. Do not leave them out. They help you grow.

Secondly, *don't let your problems and failures nag you.* It is better to look at Christ—His perfection—His love for us—His desire to cleanse and forgive us whenever we recognize sin and failure. Let Him have a chance and you will know the secret of continuous victory!*

The roadblocks pointed out in this chapter, including the sex problem, add up to the challenge that called the Campaign into existence. Never does disappointment, even the gravest, quench the courage of a Young Life worker. His sole concern continues to be that of befriending the needy, of helping to redeem those who have fallen. Whoever has heard Jim Rayburn expound the story of the woman taken in adultery cannot fail to realize how deeply effective the evangelical approach of Young Life is bound to be.

## Rewards

The history of Pat, a teen-ager from the Far West, makes an unexpected sequel to the New Testament story. The western town in which the boy was born had only a few, hardly noticeable areas of blight, but Pat had the bad luck to grow up in one of these sections of the city. His father was a "hod-carrier," that is, a laborer. His mother worked in the kitchen of the largest hotel in town, on the night shift. He had two sisters and a brother, but they were older and were gone most of the day, so that the boy had little supervision. When his parents were together they fought quite a bit; the father drank and the mother complained about it. Truly a vicious circle.

Pat was first arrested for shoplifting when he was eleven years

* *Young Life Magazine*, September 1961, p. 15.

old. He spent the night in the detention home. From that time until his junior year in high school he was in constant trouble with the police and school authorities. He had a bad temper and was always fighting, and he had learned to drink while still very young. Every one of his friends had a police record, and most of them have since gone to prison or reformatory school. More than once he had to change from one junior high school to another, because he was always in trouble.

When he entered senior high he became interested in football, but that did not last long, and he was repeatedly suspended from school. On one of these occasions (he was in trouble again for fighting) he went to the Young Life Club—in order to meet a girl! The leader was beginning to present to the youngsters the story of the woman taken in adultery. Pat found himself wondering: if Christ could love a prostitute, maybe he could love me too? That night when he went to bed he prayed that if God wanted his life he should take it, because thus far he, Pat, had made a mess of it. The Young Life leader together with a Presbyterian assistant minister began to spend a great deal of time with the new convert—who incidentally got in difficulty again for wrecking a car. But the awareness that someone cared for him saved him this time. He joined the Church and ultimately gained admission to Princeton Theological Seminary. His last word to me is characteristic of the radical change that has taken place in him: "I'll probably go into the parish ministry, but I'm open to another calling."

No wonder Young Life leaders soon forget even their greatest trials in the face of such mighty acts of deliverance. The note of love, joy, and gratitude predominates as things forgiven fade away. Lee Izmirian, writing from Pasadena, California, exults in her friendship with girls she has led to Christ. "Their freshness, spontaneity, and hunger for more knowledge about the One who dwells within, I have found highly refreshing, motivating, and rewarding." Does this mean that Lee has never been greatly tried? Of course not. It is just that, in lives she has seen, the Gospel has been allowed to have its way.

Discouraging as teen-agers may be at times, and heartbreak notwithstanding, a Young Life leader will stand up for those he loves to call his kids. He will insist that you can trust such youngsters. Mike Escalante, who gives a glowing, lively report on lads who have literally forced his admiration, quotes one of them as saying, "I don't believe in God, but if at some time during camp I can feel convinced that there is one, I will accept him." You bet he will! To accuse a fellow like this of spiritual pride would be missing the mark.

Because they realize that they are loved and trusted, teen-agers are more willing to acknowledge the truth presented to them in simplicity of heart. To this truth they will surrender, once evidence has convinced them that "this is it." Jay Grimstead, area director in the La Habra-Whittier-Downey area of Southern California, gave me a thrilling illustration of this frame of mind. He had just begun working in a club largely made up of "hoods"—that is, fellows who gain recognition, not through the usual constructive channels—athletics, cheerleading, school politics, or the like—but by destructive means such as drinking, fighting, and vandalism.

One night Jay met nine of these boys at the hamburger joint they frequented. It was then about 10 P.M. on a school night. They shared with him their latest exploit, which was running around town in their swim suits, finding a swimming pool, and jumping over the fence and swimming until someone came out of the house and told them to leave. They would then leave and repeat the stunt at the next pool they could find.

An idea immediately came to Jay's mind. He had a friend whose house and pool were open to him. Why not invite the youngsters over there for a late swim? This would mean additional contact with them, as well as stopping their wild activity. He called up his friend, who immediately agreed. The boys liked the idea. When they arrived, Jay's friend had a large pot of coffee brewing. As the evening wore on, he did not seem to notice the boys' smoking or mishandling his property. When they and the Young Life worker had swum to their heart's content, he served them coffee. The fellows were amazed that any adult could be so nice to them. They let down their tough barriers and began to show the brighter side of their personalities. They and Jay left about eleven-thirty. From then on, Jay was their older "buddy," and soon they and their girl friends had signed up for a trip to Frontier Ranch. Let no wise Christian knit his brows at this sequence of events. The Lord reigneth.

Indeed, miracles do happen when adults begin to co-operate! Roadblocks then fade away. Bob Page has a beautiful Christmas story to tell which should provide a fitting conclusion to this chapter. A Young Life Club he worked with was rather wild and sorely in need of revival. On Christmas Eve a group of teen-agers were eagerly preparing to leave the next day for snow camping at Silver Cliff Ranch. The leader was quite depressed, however, for he was ten short of a full bus. This meant not only a financial loss, but also that ten young people who direly needed the Christ would miss an opportunity of confrontation. At the time, Bob and his wife Mae Louise lived next door to an ex-alcoholic who owned a dry-cleaning business and had become a close "father-friend" to the Pages and their two children. This man—Bud—happened over that night and remarked that Bob looked down in the dumps. Bob told him about having to leave ten kids at home that needed the Lord, and when he asked why, explained that they could not afford the cost—sixty dollars each.

Bud said to him, "Could you get ten kids on this short notice if you had the money?" Bob thought he could. Right there, Bud wrote a check for six hundred dollars and told his young friend to get busy. Within two hours the Young Life leader had ten young men lined up, who could not believe that such things happened. On Christmas morning they left for Silver Cliff.

They all had a tremendous week of skiing, ice-skating, and bus-riding. Bill Starr was the camp speaker. About eight of those ten boys opened their hearts to Christ, among many others there.

During the return trip home on the bus, about three o'clock in the morning, a man who with his wife had been chaperoning their daughter at the camp leaned over Bob's seat and said, "Bob, I thought you would like to know that my wife and I understand what our daughter has, and what we have been missing. We talked it over last night, and we have opened our hearts to Christ." Their daughter had previously gone through the same experience at Malibu. Her father became the leading layman behind the local work of Young Life until his death. Since then his wife is finding consolation and purpose in life through the One whom both of them had met at Silver Cliff that Christmas week.

# 7

# NEW DIRECTIONS

## *Need of Broader Financing*

So FAR we have identified the main features of the organic solidarity of Young Life, and some problems with which it must come to grips. Over the years those features have added up to quite an impressive structural organization, considering that it has been contrived on an emergency basis. Unexpected situations compelled Jim Rayburn and his small band of early followers to improvise. New difficulties have acted as incentives to devise new resources. Throughout it all, the undaunted innovators have endured, thanks to a near-Calvinistic sense of God's sovereignty.

This tribute once paid, it should be granted that the shoestring kind of regime under which Young Life has all along had to operate has put harsh restrictions on its progress. The Campaign gets only 5 per cent of its money from foundations, and this is shocking to one who considers some of the items on which a number of them occasionally spend their funds. Operating budgets mostly come from individuals and about two hundred churches. Average gifts are small. There is no guarantee on the salary of staff members. All bills are paid first, and salaries take second place. As previously stated, the end of the fiscal year is September 30, and any salary not paid by that time is cancelled. In actual practice, miracles have occurred in this area also. God has provided, and every year except one, early in the work, the money has come in on time.

The fact remains, nevertheless, that for want of substantial reserves Young Life has had to show circumspection in selecting new areas of work among those where an immediate need had become particularly pressing. The reason for this is that the resources for each new field of activity have to be found in that area. It is up to the local committee to build a platform of adult support on which the incoming leader will stand. A program comes into existence because committeemen have wanted it and invited Young Life to come in. They must accordingly stand squarely behind it. Even if they do, unexpected circumstances may jeopardize initial efforts. Also involved in this general issue is that of recruiting an adequate personnel, in view of the fact that salaries are below average and not even guaranteed. It is sad to learn—and the inquirer has to work hard to find it out—that a large proportion of Young Life leaders have had to borrow during their lean season, in a number of cases quite heavily.

Yet the Campaign's experience in some sixty cities has shown what could happen in 500 cities with proper financing. Because the basic situation has not been fully appreciated, the insinuation has spread abroad that Young Life makes it a policy to cater to well-to-do neighborhoods—a mischievous and ill-founded rumor if there ever was one! What should have been said is that as long as Young Life lacks the financial assets that will allow more freedom of initiative, the organization has no right to imperil present commitments. Expansion cannot as yet be based solely on the degree of felt need. This, however, does not mean that slum areas have been shunned or that tough individuals and sordid situations have not been met, and squarely. To that, the preceding pages have already borne witness. What will shortly be said on the Star Ranch experiment, and also a recent thrust into the asphalt jungles of Newark and New York City, should further vindicate the Campaign if need be. It will then appear that the kind of probing that brought the movement into existence is as diligent and unwearied as ever.

## Asphalt Jungle and Tree-lined Street

Admittedly, about 95 per cent of Young Life's present activity is in the suburban "typically American" setting. Rennie MacKay, who works in an Illinois town, tells me that although she has had some "terribly disappointing experiences," one does stand out in her memory. It concerns a girl from a very sad home background—an alcoholic father, very little love in the family, and few friends. Although the girl craved love and friendship, she never was able to accept the fact that Jesus could love her. Instead, she shut herself off from the One who would have given her the love she had been searching for. A moving story—nay, one in which man's eternal plight is epitomized. Yet its very setting and presentation—as standing out among major disappointments—would suggest that Rennie has not thus far had to contend with evil in its most virulent aspects.

The ways and means of teen-age evangelization already presented may indeed be said to have been worked out on the economic level of the middle class and upper-middle class. At this level, the structure of today's teen-age society has not as yet set into its hard core. Activities which would be considered mere horseplay in the exclusive gangs of crowded tenements make banner headlines in the social set of Gopher Prairie. Rick Yates, Young Life area director in Bremerton, Washington, was greatly concerned—and rightly—when one of his club's backsliders managed to obtain the key and steal about $900 in bonds from his mother's safe deposit box, and bought a car. He kept the car hidden and his mother only discovered the theft when she came to consult with Rick about her son; Rick mentioned the car to her, thinking she had allowed the lad to buy it. He had neither driver's license nor insurance. Rick sought him out and lovingly tried to help him. The boy showed no sign of sorrow. The car was finally sold. Later the culprit moved out of his family house and started living with a friend in an apartment. He left school and has not been heard from since.

Suppose we now move on to the asphalt jungle and transpose this incident to the current practices of real "tough guys." What we get then is no longer an episodic brush with a law-abiding citizenry, but a new code of morality. Four teen-agers recently admitted stealing three late-model automobiles. They stripped the cars, sold the parts, and used the proceeds to "soup up" their own hot rods. One teen-ager mentioned by Ray M. King, manager of the National Auto Theft Bureau, thus boasted that he could remove a car's trasmission, (worth about $250) in eight minutes. About a thousand cars are stolen every day in the United States, and judging from previous experience the FBI estimates that teen-agers may be responsible for approximately 65 per cent of that figure.

Why this sordid situation? Teen-agers admittedly have financial problems. Unemployment among those who quit school is high. Yet motivation strikes deeper; says Mr. King—and he ought to know, since his bureau is supported by about 350 insurance companies— "A lot of teen-agers steal cars because they think it's the smart thing to do; it shows their pals they are not 'chicken.' " That is, they steal cars for the same sort of reason as gives them a spurious sense of strength from the motor's roar, or makes them feel their girls are impressed when the noise climaxes in "gunning."

The new generation of teen-agers confronted by Young Life in areas walled in by crowded tenements calls for new research and experimentation on the part of its leaders. Thus far, the Campaign has had to cope mostly with the "typically American" fellow. Phil McDonald, area director in Minneapolis, characterizes him in a colorful sketch—actually of one of his own teen-agers who had led him through the whole gamut of a leader's experience:

He was typical of thousands of fellas in our American high schools. He seldom went to church—only a few times a year. He was a terrific athlete —first-string fullback—a bruising, powerful kid. He was notorious for his quick temper. Nobody ever crossed him if they were smaller—not too many tried if they were bigger. He won more than his share of fights.

And of course he got dead drunk on occasion.

The city jungle type of teen-ager, on the other hand, is found in a crowd—in a famous gang of he-men if he turns out to be a somebody. Since he has nowhere else to go, his hangout is the sidewalk. He may occasionally smile, but not a smile of hope; there is nothing for him to hope for. Under a crushing weight of boredom or a craving for popularity at any cost, he will attempt the craziest feats, such as breaking open a hydrant and shooting beer cans on the stream of water. When his pent-up feelings are too much to be relieved by horseplay, or the thought of an empty future proves unbearable, or grim pressure from the gang gets irresistible, a shot of heroin becomes the temptation—soon the addiction.

There is actually at work in the contemporary teen-ager an urge to experiment with intoxication. I do not refer here to alcohol (although according to FBI statistics, in 1961, 104,174 teen-agers were arrested for drunkenness, driving while intoxicated, and generally violating liquor laws—a figure greater than the total number of arrests of teen-agers for robbery, all types of assault, prostitution, other sex offenses, gambling, and narcotics violations combined). My point is the increasing use of any kind of substance that works as a narcotic.

The latest fad in this regard has been glue-sniffing, an addiction that damages vital organs and may even cause death. The youngsters squeeze model glue into cloths, and inhale. The fumes from quick-drying solvents in the glue, such as toluene and acetone, produce an intoxicating effect which is likely to lead to violence. There is, for example, the well-authenticated case of a fourteen-year-old boy in a Southern California town who sniffed five tubes of glue a day. He recently attacked a woman and forced her out of her car, then drove off and smashed into three others. To pass "anti-sniffing" laws as three Southern California towns (Anaheim, Azusa, and Woodland) have already done, obviously does not reach to the roots of the situation. The new teen-age structures which are now coming into their own in semi-depleted areas, and in the concrete jungle of many of our major cities, call for the sort of creativity and freshness of approach which has allowed the Campaign effectively to reach teen-agers at the middle-class and upper-middle-class level.

## Star Ranch Experiment

The kind of probing which in the first place produced Young Life is being pursued with added supervision and assistance. During the summer of 1962, three weeks of the Star Ranch calendar were subsidized and set aside for youngsters from the tenements of a half-dozen large cities. Juvenile officers and professors of sociology were in attendance as observers. William E. Milliken, who took twenty-eight boys and twelve girls from New York City to the camp, characterizes his experience as one of witnessing one miracle after another. One of the first miracles, as he sees it, was the easy and successful trip. Only once did any problem arise with color prejudice, and that was in a small town in Iowa. Fortunately there were no incidents. The emergency merely provided a fresh opportunity for the group to discuss the problem with the leaders. Conversely, the leaders had a chance to get acquainted with some of the youngsters they had hardly met before. Barriers between the New York boys and those from other cities were also broken down.

In true Young Life style, the leaders' testimonies added up to a great feeling of humility at the realization of their own helplessness. Also to an increased dependence upon the Holy Spirit. What happened as the experiment progressed called forth awed wonder on their part. Take the case of the boy they called Tap, for instance—an eighteen-year-old from the Smith projects in New York and one of the most-followed individuals on the lower East Side. The miracle of his being "broken up" on the third night of camp helped transform the lives of the roughest kids who had come to the ranch. What created this situation was an incident that brought Tap to a showdown with Bill Milliken, in charge of the expedition. By God's grace, the two did not come to blows. Instead, Bill was given the opportunity of explaining to Tap that his big problem was that of pride, and that Christ could change this. Bill actually gave Tap every reason in the world to slug him; but instead of hitting him, Tap admitted to his need of Christ. The transformation of his life since that day has also been a miracle.

His remaining great fear was that of having to face his crowd as a changed person. One of the great uses of the camp—as in religious retreats—is to isolate young people long enough from the negative, mask-requiring pressures of their lives to allow them to find their true selves, and to gain the courage to stand firm later.

Another tremendous transformation occurred in the life of a fellow known by the name of Boots, a twenty-two-year-old Negro boy from the same project. He was chief of a gang known as the Social Jesters, a clique of youngsters between eighteen and twenty-four. They were actually the controlling and ruling group of all the cliques in this housing development. Boot was the roughest guy who had been brought to the ranch. All week long he claimed that he could not bow to Christ because of what it would cost him personally, and because it would hurt his position in the city. Yet on the very last night of camp, Boot stood up before his crowd to say he had surrendered to the Lord. It must have taken a lot of nerve for him to do that.

A similar experience was that of another eighteen-year-old boy, a member of a group known as the Cavaliers and the "key guy of the gang." When he first came to the ranch, he admitted he was there just for a good time and did not care to hear about religion. About halfway through the week, he was really listening. Then came his admission that he was confused, actually aware of a need in his life. The day before camp was over, he came to the leader and said he wanted to ask Christ into his life.

Still another lad, known as Butch, opened his heart to God on the way home. His words are worth quoting: "I opened the lock to the door and God has come in—and I close it now for he won't ever leave me."

Three girls, each a key member of her clique, met Christ in a real, personal way. Two of them are Puerto Rican, the other a Negro.

Terry Olsen, of Young Life in San Leandro, California, was a counselor at this experimental Star Ranch camp. What impressed him most, according to a letter just received, was that somehow the youngsters realized that their only real chance was at hand. Their life's contention every day was with dope, the curse of overcrowded tenements, and all the forces of evil that threatened to blot them out. Their parole officers should probably be added to the list of what they felt themselves contending against, for it required patient negotiation with the powers of the law to bring them to Colorado. The concluding paragraph of Terry's letter is touching.

I hear about every ten days from a Negro boy who was with the group that came to Star Ranch this summer. We formed quite an attachment for each other, and it was my privilege to be his counselor in his decision to trust the Lord. We write back and forth to one another, and what a joy to read how he is going on with the Lord, and how excited he is about the Christian life. It is heart-warming. (He is being followed up by our Young Life workers in this area.)

But, some will object, one can count these converts on the fingers of his hand! Possibly. Pete Bennett, who was only able to bring one fellow out of the six he had lined up in a Texas town, assured me that what had happened to this one erased his disappointment at having missed the others. For several months he has been an assest to his family, school, and community. It is possible for one redeemed life, Pete concluded, to affect the life of an entire school.

What then shall we say of the transformed lives of these most-followed individuals and gang leaders of lower Manhattan in New York City?

## Young Life in the Big City

The pioneering thus far done on the lower East Side of New York by a Young Life leader of the caliber of Bill Milliken is astonishing and augurs well for the Young Life of tomorrow. It gives an idea of what can be done in the most strenuous, most demanding circumstances, among teen-agers hemmed in by the powers of evil our age has let loose.

The atmosphere of the great city jungles is one of stale smells, soulless sounds, and faded hopes. It is as though no useful contact could ever be made in an environment of that kind. Bill told me that for a long time any attempt, any sort of approach, seemed sheer vanity. During one span of four months, between November, 1961 through February, 1962, everything previously done literally fell apart. It seemed as if the innumerable hours spent, day and night, over the preceding two years with one fellow after another had been wholly wasted. Streets and dark alleys took their toll; gang pressure did its damage. Fellows who had begun to see the light were sucked back by the prevailing forces of evil. Alcohol and narcotics knocked off even the most promising lads.

At this juncture the first great lesson was learned, or perhaps one should say learned afresh, for the truth from which it derives was one of the very first articles of faith of Young Life. Yet more than mere recovery was involved—namely, a new creative development. In Bill's own words,

We were frustrated on all sides, disheartened, and almost defeated. Christ had truly broken us; we were forced to our knees in endless hours of prayer! Our Lord had taught us one big truth. If the work was to go on, and progress in lives was to be made, this would have to be *his work* and not ours. The learning of this truth was the beginning of victory.

Christ made me realize that if gang activity was to be broken up because certain individuals met Christ, a structure as dynamic as the gang would need to be set up to fulfill the needs of these "new creatures in Christ." For as long as they fought the battle as individuals only, they became easy prey to the great forces of sin around them. I found that the typical Young Life Campaigner methods met needs, but this was not enough in this situation. Something more tangible and challenging had to be formed.

This indeed *was* a fresh discovery. Bill's finding was in line with the Campaign's innermost convictions, but it also implied a new step forward. There was in it the freshness of creativity. From here on, ways and means as yet untried were in the making. Once more, as he took the initiative, the Young Life tradition of adult leadership was upheld and sustained. Yet the innovation that was to come out of it broke new ground.

Bill was led to talk to nine young men about the possibility of uniting for Christ in a disciplined manner. He warned each individual that this would really be hard, the hardest thing they had ever set out to do. Incidentally, he proved a shrewd psychologist at this point. One may safely lay down the principle that the average youngster is eager to tackle difficulty and ready to rise to the occasion. He is earnest about it. To try to allure him through facility can only make for flabbiness, and we have too much of such defeatism in America today. Not so Bill Milliken. He told the nine boys that the Christian life was not an easy thing but a battle, and that they would wage it on the roughest of battlefields. He added that anything they set out to do would prove impossible without the power of Christ pouring through each one of them, and quoted Scripture to prove his point. Five of the boys responded to the challenge. They called themselves the Cross Carriers.

The early weeks were difficult, yet highly stimulating. There were stumbling blocks. First, the five were of completely different personal types. Moreover, four were Puerto Rican; the fifth a Negro. They came from different gangs and neighborhoods—two were the president and vice-president of the Young Dragons, one belonged in the Imperial Dragon territory, one came from the Smith projects, and one from a neighborhood at the other end of the lower East Side.

The second hindrance was that they were not used to discussing as a group. And third, each was on a different level of growth in the Christian life.

Bill had taken the initiative. The boys proceeded to thrash out difficulties somewhat on their own terms, and it was at this point that new ground was further opened up. If the five youngsters were to make any headway as a unit, they needed a constitution. So they planned and drafted one themselves. No legalism was involved in this; essentially it represented a felt need for a set of living standards and goals with regard to their Christian profession. The Constitution of the Cross Carriers was voted and approved on May 17, 1962 and appeared under the motto, "If any man will come after me, let him deny himself, and take up his cross daily, and follow me" (Luke 9:23). The charter was divided into two sets of rules, one concerning the discipline of members and the other concerning growth in the Christian life. The document cannot be truly appreciated unless one keeps in mind the fact that it has been drafted by the lower East Side boys themselves.

Under "Discipline of Members" there were rules concerning attendance, with fines implied; narcotics—not to be used in any form, otherwise the culprit would be dismissed from the club; work and school—a member must be either working, looking for work, or going to school; tithing—pledge of a quarter a week toward helping others, and if a member misses paying a week, he must pay double the following week; honesty, expected at all times—honesty with God, with oneself, and with the group; fighting—no member is expected to "bop" at any time; profanity—refrain from cursing at all times; drinking—left at the discretion of the individual, provided he does not drink around the park, or ever get drunk; purity—modeled on Christ's example. Penalties for breaking any rule—to be left in the hands of the other members.

Under "Growth in the Christian Life" were such specifications as these: one verse must be learned each week; each member must have his own Bible; he is expected to study it daily and to discuss briefly once a week what he has learned during the preceding week; he must submit to testing on the material the adviser has covered, and keep his notebook up to date. He should attend either church or Sunday school each week.

Appended "Important Notes" show at the outset that the Cross Carriers are in the true Young Life tradition. The club, according to Note I, "is founded on and centered in the person of Jesus Christ." (Though one senses here an educated wording, it was wording the boys themselves had taken up.) Note II insists that "each member must have a personal relationship and daily walk with Jesus Christ." Note III echoes the Constitution's New Testament motto by stating that the club's key Bible verse is Luke 9:23, while Note IV points to Romans 12 as the fraternity's key chapter. The names of the charter members appear under Note V, and the document comes to a close with this moving statement, "If Jesus Christ be God and died for me, then no sacrifice I make for him will be too great."

The typical Cross Carrier meeting begins with a prayer, after which current business matters and general problems are discussed and adequate decisions made. Then Bill as the adviser goes around and evaluates members one by one, first mentioning areas of their life in which there is need for improvement, then commending them in areas where they have improved. But then, as behooves a group of genuine disciples, each member in turn applies the same treatment to the leader himself, not forgetting those areas where he, too, needs to improve!

At this point also a new trail is being blazed. Does this mean that the Young Life of tomorrow is likely to be half-leader, half-teen-ager centered? Perhaps to borrow some of the ways of Alcoholics Anonymous? I wonder. There follows a general time of being honest with each other, confessing various difficulties and actual sins—indeed, a typical AA feature. What has been gained from Bible study by each individual is shared with the others, with particular reference to the Lord's work in one's life. Things that need to be prayed for are surveyed. A half-hour to an hour is further spent in prayer. The meeting is brought to a close with Bible study or a period of instruction by the leader.

Those who may be tempted to minimize the importance of small beginnings had better inquire into the ways the Lord has used the Cross Carriers. Before the group was started there was in the regular club only one Negro boy who knew the Lord; aside from him, only a few of the twenty or thirty kids that came were Negro. The majority were Puerto Rican. Up to the starting of the Cross Carriers, Bill and his fellow workers had been averaging twelve to fifteen youngsters at the Sunday school class they had organized in a lower East Side church. (Incidentally, the age of these boys is between fifteen and twenty-four). Mainly through the efforts of the five initial Cross Carriers, forty youngsters were at hand when time came to leave for the summer of 1962. There at the ranch, each of the Cross Carriers could see friends, whom they had been working with and praying for, meet the Lord. A month later, four Negro boys and two Puerto Ricans had been added to the fraternity. At the time of this writing, the Cross Carriers are eleven in number and hard at work. The Young Life

Club itself averages in the seventies and eighties, while the Sunday school has doubled in size.

What matters more than statistics, however, is the tremendous transformation that has taken place in the individual Cross Carriers. Each one is working with and praying for an outside friend. One fellow has Bible study with as many as twelve of his former gang members every week.

When such things happen on the lower East Side of New York City, new horizons may be said to have opened up for the translation of New Testament evangelism into a mission to modern teen-agers, such as the Young Life Campaign initiated. New emphases come into their own.

## Outside the U.S.A.

I have barely mentioned the movement in Canada, and little will be said here of the new and exciting development of Young Life in other countries. These are fresh beginnings and accordingly in a state of flux. It was my privilege in the summer of 1963 to discuss the over-all planning for work in France with Rod Johnson and Marc Atger, who will share the directorship, and that long consultation confirmed my view that foreign developments as whole, though very interesting, should be allowed to crystallize before an attempt is made to treat them at any length.

Nevertheless, Young Life clubs are taking shape in Europe, from Paris (four clubs in the suburbs) to Frankfort-am-Main and beyond. Especially in France and West Germany, teen-age camps and leadership seminars are in process of development. A permanent "ranch" in the French Alps is being planned. It is fascinating to think of high-school students journeying recently from both France and Germany to the mountains of Switzerland for a camping period with leaders Rod Johnson, Paris representative, and Johnny O'Neil from Germany. A Swiss ski instructor who met the Young Life people wrote with feeling "I'll exert myself to keep in contact with people who trust God so much." Or again, imagine a busload of sixty-five

French youngsters hearing the New Testament proclaimed in a new key during an Easter weekend in Belgium!

It is noteworthy that the French for "Young Life" is "Jeunesse Ardente"— that is, "Youth Aglow" or "Youth Aflame." Yet the youngsters' response (not to speak of their parents) is sometimes negative. Problems arise—that of financing, for instance—which call for new solutions. While tested methods of approach to the young people are used abroad, their flexibility allows a high degree of adaptation to national and local situations. There is an awareness, for example, of stricter parental control; thus when George Sheffer was sent to Europe by headquarters, he spoke not only at camp meetings but at "parents' nights." The special tastes of European youngsters provide fresh opportunities, as when over four hundred adolescents gathered in a Paris concert hall by invitation of the Campaign to hear Negro spirituals and classical music along with the vibrant testimonies of recent converts, climaxed by a short Gospel message.

In South America attention is being concentrated on Brazil, where the pressures of widespread, bitter poverty have tended to drive young people out of highly formal religious life into the arms of radical social movements. No field is more in need of truly Christian dedication, fellowship, and service. The task of exploration is being guided by men deeply versed in South American ways and in the Christian mission—men of the caliber of Millard R. Shaull and John A. Mackay. A co-ordinated study of the field has already reached an advanced stage.

# 8

# THE WAY AHEAD

*Toward Christian Service*

THOSE WHO ARE in a position to see for themselves what is being accomplished under the auspices of the adult leadership of Young Life cannot help asking, How do they do it? I have already quoted Roy Riviere, Jim's executive assistant, to the effect that whatever is done is a matter neither of program nor of materials. Jim himself steadily refuses to see his staff promote any stereotyped way for coming to Christ, or recommend any kind of experience. To him the very word "technique" is anathema. I heard him at the 1963 Leaders Conference for the Northeast and Southeast ardently draw attention to the fact that Jesus never once duplicated his approach to individuals. He did not treat even two blind men alike. Was one then to imagine Young Life devising a technique for the evangelization of blind men and issuing a manual on the subject—?

From the very beginning, Young Life has dealt with every single human situation on its own merit. The vitality of the movement may accordingly be ascribed in part to its flexibility. The Campaign has mostly proceeded by trial and error, to the point of being dubbed empirical in its approach. One of the main reasons for this practice is not far to seek, although it goes all the way back to Jim's Arizona days when he laid his hands on Chafer's book, *He That Is Spiritual*. Young Life relies on the Holy Spirit. "We believe in leaving this up to the Holy Spirit," is one of Jim's stock utterances. The Campaign should never be allowed to harden into an institutional setup.

As the preceding chapters have shown, staff members display an amazing ingenuity in securing the attention of teen-agers. Every decent kind of approach is acceptable, provided it leads to the goal. Mal McSwain, who works in Charlotte, North Carolina, characterizes this goal in clear-cut terms: ". . . to see a teen-ager with no religious background respond to my friendship, warm up to Christian realities, commit his life to Christ, become active in a church, continue to personally grow in Christ, help another person find his Savior, be consistent through college."

In the school of hard knocks, Young Life leaders are learning further that, while coddling may help in the early stages of approach to teen-agers, one must not indulge in too much of it. Admittedly, a measure of pampering may be permissible at the outset to persuade the fellows to come to club or go to camp and to make them feel happy there. But surely, once they have begun to tread the narrow path, such coddling should yield to more mature ways—essentially to such ways of self-denial and Christian service as have become current practice in the New York lower East Side experiment, and indeed, already in a number of areas where the Young Life effort has become manifest.

Campaign leaders need not be told that, while believing the truth is important, to *do* the truth is what ultimately matters. The faith they proclaim is not merely a subject to talk about or even pray over. It is a reality upon which one proceeds. "By their fruits ye shall know them"—here ends the spoken word. Here ends the glowing week in camp or the public confession of faith at club or among the Campaigners. But only he or she who *does* the truth shall come to the light, and most likely continue to dwell in it. The reason we can do nothing without the Lord is that in him, and in him alone, do we find the knowing *and* the doing identified.

I was once reminded of this Young Life emphasis as I passed by a movie theater. An elderly lady stood there looking at a poster of what was "now playing." The show had to do with certain aspects of our teen-agers' plight. The youngsters insolently pictured in rather lurid colors were obviously on the rampage. A subtitle suggested that what was to be seen on the screen would help one understand their condition. For a while the old lady held her sharply outlined chin upraised toward the poster, then slowly moved on, mumbling, "Give them some work to do!" A wise remark, which should please those concerned at the high rate of unemployment among teen-agers who quit school. But somehow I do not believe she meant it that way. Her tone, as I remember the scene, referred rather to what one might characterize as the expulsive power of a call to service.

That very call is what is now heard more loudly and clearly among boys and girls won to Christ under the auspices of the Young Life Campaign. The way ahead points in that direction. Freely granting the desirability and relevance of clubs, Campaigner groups, and summer ranches, we may look forward to hearing about the youngsters' stationing some of their number at volunteer posts; we may expect to be told of their readiness to answer an alert—whether this be an emergency request for help to a needy widow, a family in distress, an afflicted community, or even a disaster area. Or bear in mind simply the example of the Cross Carriers, initiating Bible study with former fellow gang members, as the dross that may yet have lingered in their redeemed souls yields further to the expulsive power of a call to Christian service.

## College Follow-up

The way ahead for Young Life points to yet a further call, namely, perseverance in new-found faith once high-school days are over and college begins. Ahead lies the possibility of a crisis for youngsters thus far nurtured by Young Life. I hardly need emphasize that this college crisis is not peculiar to them alone. Any young Christian is bound sooner or later to be affected by it. Although an impressive number of the Young Life converts that have come out of some of our leading colleges and universities have gone on to a growing, dynamic and vigorous Christian life, others have had a change of heart. There has been falling away; there has been involvement in contrary fraternities; the rebellious attitude of unbelievers has proved contagious and has undermined faith. Here also, as Young Life faces the way ahead, its leaders need to pause and give further consideration to the plight of some of its young people in trouble.

A career spent in college, university, and then in seminary teaching, has made me realize that students mostly change their minds because they have had access to fresh information. In a number of cases the outcome of this experience has been nothing short of a disruption of their whole outlook on life, and this is indeed serious business for any thoughtful, responsible fellow. The landscape of reality apprehended in college no longer squares with that formerly viewed from the angle of the high-school campus in the days of the Young Life Club.

But there is infinitely more at stake in the crisis undergone by a college student than a matter of Biblical cosmology: namely, the total impact of a liberal arts education mostly bent on the naturalistic way. At this point, philosophers and scientists assume the appraiser's role from their professorial chairs. On occasion they even take the measure of Biblical views. The professor of religion himself may turn out to be quite upsetting to a candid teen-ager fresh from the Young Life Club. Neither will this boy or girl find comfort in a retreat toward so-called "unformulated experiences." Anthropologists, sociologists, psychologists, psychoanalysts, pathologists, and even biochemists of the glands will invade the scene now their own and proceed to explain away whatever may be left of these experiences, once the survey is concluded. What is a Christian teen-ager to do? Young Life leaders confronted by the college man's change of attitude are well aware that it will not avail them to complain at this point, or even to cast some campus figure or group in the role of villain. Neither will they emulate those who point out that Satan must have made today's college or university campus the private hunting ground of his greatest predilection.

It is fair to say that, generally speaking, the issue of college follow-up is attracting increased attention in Young Life circles these days. Thus it is my understanding that a distinguished and highly qualified Yale Divinity School graduate may soon be entrusted with research and subsequent recommendations on the subject. He is thoroughly familiar with Young Life, for he met Christ at the club George Sheffer used to conduct on the Chicago North Shore.

My own view on this matter of college crisis is that, while Young Life should continue to focus its interest on high-school students, special effort should be made by its leaders to relate their action to that of college and university chaplains. These men are after all especially trained to take care of the Christian follow-up work that may be needed. Moreover, in a large number of institutions campus chaplains are—as are Young Life leaders—interdenominational either in fact or in emphasis. Why could not some such representative as the president of the Young Life Institute or a member of his faculty make at least a yearly visit on campus, perhaps at the request of the students themselves? Such an undertaking should prove both acceptable to the college or university authorities and valuable to the students involved.

One may follow this up with the suggestion that, as Young Life looks at the way ahead, its leaders themselves have an obligation to play a part in this matter of college reconnoitering. In their preparation for future tasks they are continually bringing their own college and seminary training up to date. All now begin on the full-time Young Life staff as trainees. The appointee who brings to the job a college degree can anticipate a minimum of three and a half years on the trainee staff, during which he will both gain field experience and complete the degree program at the Young Life Institute. A man (or woman) who brings a seminary degree, on the other hand, can anticipate a minimum of one year as a trainee, during which he will have a taste of field experience and take two Institute courses.

## The Institute and Future Program

However intensive its accelerated program, the summer Institute continues to look forward to a most demanding task, if the problem of reconception henceforth thrust upon Young Life is to be met. The Institute's faculty stands prepared, being made up of men—good scholars, all—drawn from various institutions (colleges, universities, and seminaries). Yet, though there are among them varying degrees of familiarity with Young Life, on the whole there is still little consensus of opinion with regard to the Institute's relatedness to the total program of the Campaign. For example, in actual practice, professors invited to teach a subject called for by the curriculum are likely to use material pertaining to their own field of interest—material organized in such ways as to fit into the context of another institution's needs. It is possible that offerings thus compounded may well, and occasionally do, conflict in their assumptions, without there being either time or opportunity for essential seminar discussion and reconsideration.

A further difficulty lies in the uneven preparation of the students who rub elbows in the same classroom. Some, for instance, may have "taken religion" in college; others may be attending the Institute merely to supplement a theological education received from a leading seminary. In these circumstances, it is difficult for a professor to discern indispensable common ground. The very aims of individual students differ. Some may be preparing themselves to serve a certain denomination; others—and these are in the majority—are mostly concerned with the minimum academic work required for membership on the staff.

Uncertainty as to purpose is hardly dispelled by an Institute catalog now on my desk in which the training program is presented as "a contribution to the total work of the Church." However meritorious, this last statement is confusing to say the least. Could it be, then, that the well-intentioned organizers of the Young Life Summer Institute have erred in trying to be everything to everyone in a couple of summer months—even twice repeated?

The fact is, we may remember, that the Institute was at its very inception conceived on a year-round basis. As some of us used to say not so long ago, "There's a war on!" The Army, the Navy, and the Air Force have their training centers. So, incidentally, has the Salvation Army. Why not Young Life?

Only a unified program can be unifying. The vision without which the people perish must come from the top, that is, from the Board of Directors and from "the boss," as the Executive Director is affectionately known. The permanent Institute faculty they would select would be a Young Life faculty. Once well integrated as a team, its members would concur in one design—a design for the Young Life of the future. This would then eventually be further worked out at joint meetings of the faculty and Board of Directors presided over by the Executive Director. Thus would fresh blood be infused into the Young Life leadership as a whole. It may be assumed that, after a period of time, the purposive planning which had thus been formulated and agreed upon would increasingly permeate the Campaign and reshape it along firmer lines. In such a setting, the adult leadership which has all along characterized Young Life would truly come into its own. The Young Life Campaign of the future must be more vigorously integrated without losing any of its flexibility and adaptability. Only the truly strong are in a position to lay a gentle hand on critical issues.

## Public Relations

Although Young Life may be said to endure solely in consequence of the living power of its faith, it must nonetheless come to terms with problems of public relations. The root of these problems lies in the irresistible and stubborn fact that any local Young Life program needs acceptance in the community. The new Young Life leader must accordingly be wise as a serpent, and use a great deal of persuasion and sweet reasonableness in his relationships. Every contact he makes is bound to either strengthen or weaken his position, and so condition his freedom to work with high-school students.

Since most of his activity is to take place around the school, it is important that the leader and members of the local committee make every effort short of compromise to win the confidence of the school authorities. Acceptance should prove fairly simple to secure, since the Young Life leader does not ask for any special privilege such as the use of school facilities or school time. Educators will have to be shown that Young Life is not a pressure group seeking advantage or attempting to meddle in the operation of the school program. Most of them want to be sure their youngsters are not being wrongly influenced. It is possible, also, that they need to be reassured as to the use of undue or undesirable emotional pressure on young people. Young Life policy is very clear on this score, as is its practice.

In the long run, public opinion is likely to influence the attitude of school authorities. It is highly desirable, therefore, that Young Life be known and respected by community leaders and parents alike. Acceptance by parents is particularly helpful in eliminating negative attitudes. Experience shows that the best antidote for such negativism is widespread information as to what Young Life is, who runs it, and who stands behind it. If parents have opportunities to meet the staff leader and members of the local committee—to visit a Young Life Club and drop in on a weekend or snow camp or become familiar with the summer ranching program—they will usually welcome Young Life. In the fullness of time they may even become ardent supporters with a personal story to tell. On many occasions it has been a parent's word that stopped an antagonistic move in the community.

Making ample allowance for the wisdom, training, and experience required before a Young Life leader can be really free in his work with high-school students, it should be noted that this does not essentially affect the New Testament pattern here at stake. Quite the contrary. By far the best thing a Young Life leader can do is to follow the example of noninvolvement in matters of purely secular concern that has characterized Christians on the march throughout the ages. Did not Jesus' own detachment point out the way? It is only the detached self that is capable of effective attachment.

## Understanding with the Churches

Can it be that the lower East Side experiment should be viewed as a straw in the wind, and that the regular church attendance, together with the participation in Sunday school work involved in that venture, portend closer and more friendly relations between Young Life and the churches? So it would seem, as our attention is drawn to a still unheralded attempt at *rapprochement* quite recently initiated by Jim Rayburn. It is, of course, too early to assess possible results. Thus far, the efforts of men of good will may be said to have allowed rather the detection of shoals and ridges of rocks than the mapping out of a way to the Delectable Country still on the pilgrim's horizon. Yet there is a hope in the air of better things to come.

This is how Jim Rayburn presented the matter at a symposium in Colorado Springs between the staff of *Eternity* magazine and Young Life representatives:

Recently, in a conference with pastors and educators from fourteen denominations, we began to explore a plan to provide . . . simplicity and concentration in confronting the secular world with the basics of the faith. We came to the happy conclusion that we must begin by going back to the simple New Testament concept of the fellowship of believers. The "beloved community" must gather around the Lord Jesus for mutual encouragement and strength. Then it must move into the secular world with one idea taking pre-eminence—we are here to make Jesus Christ known. We agreed to attempt an outreach along this line— first, concerned pastors in selected communities meeting in this primitive fellowship; second, a group of lay leaders recruited by these pastors meeting in the same way for training in a loving, friendly, patient, person-to-person outreach in the unchurched community.*

Yet considerable difficulties remain. Although the conference alluded to by Jim Rayburn had brought together "pastors and educators from fourteen denominations," these only attended in a private capacity, as guests of Young Life. No official conversation between the churches and the Campaign was involved, but merely a preliminary exploration among men of good will. I spoke a while back of the subsequent detection of "shoals and ridges of rocks," and I should now come to specifics about these, at least so far as one may without violating "important prohibitions." Incidentally, the very secrecy which continues to surround the exploration at hand sufficiently indicates the ticklish character of the uphill work involved.

Let us first recall that a large section of the denominational minis-

* From *Eternity* magazine, June 1963, pp. 35f.

try still questions the very relevance of a special ministry to un-churched adolescents, the outreach to unchurched *masses* being con-sidered the real problem. That is, the very reason for Young Life's existence as an organization per se is questioned.

It would appear that what is all along left out of consideration, in such a context, is an irresistible and stubborn fact to which I have already drawn attention: namely, the division of social labor and especially its advanced stage in our contemporary society. Just as the family doctor is disappearing before the onrush of an army of spe-cialists, the minister who used to marry youngsters he had baptized and personally seen through Sunday school is also on the way out. On the one side, we now see medical patients treated on the assembly line, as it were. Blood tests, electrocardiograms, fluoroscope and X-ray examinations merely mark the initial steps, and each is in the hands of a specialist. On the other hand, when it comes to Christian life we now have a ministry of education, a ministry of visitation, a ministry in industry—even a ministry in national parks; we have the chaplaincy in prisons, in colleges, in the Army, the Navy, and the Air Force. Some ministers specialize in psychoanalysis, others in labor relations. How preposterous, therefore, the contention that such a specialized ministry as has been designed by Young Life for adolescents is not needed—and this at the very time the Campaign proves successful beyond all expectations!

Would anyone for a moment suggest that the clock be turned back—that specialists in the realm of medicine revert to general practice; or the Salvation Army, for instance, be reintegrated into the Methodist Church? It is sheer vanity to kick against the pricks of an accelerated division of social labor in every realm. Wordsworth's indignation at the sight of factory chimneys and the sound of loco-motive whistles can hardly be said to have slowed down the wheels of so-called progress. Ruskin's protests, in the name of art, against a con-spiracy of desecration that made the countryside dirty and its people ugly did not prove any more successful. Where are those who have heeded the voice of these lonely souls—except for the late Gandhi as he sat at his spinning wheel?

These pages, I hope, have shown beyond the shadow of a doubt that Young Life is meeting a dire need in the kind of world now thrust upon us. The question then is, What is likely to be the status of the Campaign as far as the churches are concerned? It has been suggested on the part of a well-intentioned clergy that Young Life might possibly be regarded as a missionary society and accordingly acknowledged by denominations. Church people could then, with their pastor's blessing, co-operate with the Campaign. Still another idea has been that Young Life may be likened to one of those Roman Catholic orders which never become substitutes for the Church but operate with the Vatican's sanction. That is, they are allowed to serve the Church so long as they do not run amok or go overboard. Such views, to say the least, would seem to reflect too condescending an attitude.

To suggest further, as some well-intentioned people are doing, that the leaders thus far produced by Young Life had best merge with Church leaders to pick out and train dedicated couples for outreach to outsiders, is merely to advocate the addition of a few drops to a monumental bucket—drops that would be seen no more, without in the least affecting the contents of the bucket over the course of time. Suppose the handful of early Salvationists had been drafted by Methodist leaders to help in the training of volunteer missionaries to the down-and-outs of their day. The clearest outcome of such an action cannot be doubted: there would be no Salvation Army now. One can hardly believe that Methodism would be different because of the supposed draft; and think of what our world would be missing if the Salvation Army were not with us!

## A *Specialized Identity*

The task at hand for Young Life is to be fruitful and multiply; to tend the fellowship of the lonely outsider, the fraternity of lost adolescents. For lo, it was not so long ago that these were the little ones Jesus insisted the world could not get along without—more than nine millions of them! Too many teen-agers just keep away from churches. And yet these same young people happen to respond to Young Life. This is the undeniable fact. Does it prove too hard to swallow for some of our clergymen? But this would spell out sheer jealousy on their part! Ought any committed Christian to resent the youngsters' keen interest in a campaign that means real life to them? I admit that they are likely to chuckle with a wink of understanding when they hear Jim's oft-quoted dictum, "It is a sin to bore kids when you talk to them about Jesus Christ." But are there many Sunday schools in the land that have not indulged in that sin?

The point I wish to stress is that, should Young Life ever lose its identity—should its workers and leaders in some way or other be absorbed by, or assimilated to, the staff of any church, group of churches, or denomination—the over-all situation would merely revert to what it was before Jim Rayburn initiated the Campaign. In this case also, the clearest, most visible outcome would be the fading away of Young Life. No one would benefit; there would be only losers on every side.

A careful consideration of the situation at hand has led me to the sober judgment that, whatever else Young Life may do in the future, it should first and foremost *preserve its identity*. Indeed, the best way for the Campaign to help any church or group of churches—or any person, for that matter—is to be its true self. Only by safeguarding its identity can the organization be in a position to co-operate genuinely with its brethren for the sake of the "beloved community" now gathering about the Lord Jesus Christ for mutual understanding and strength, in love.

Let Young Life *be* Young Life.

I vividly remember hearing, or rather, *seeing* the evangelist Gipsy Smith speak on the theme, "Let the beauty of Jesus be seen in me." This theme might well be made Young Life's own in a glow of fulfillment. Indeed, the Campaign's blessings are shed over multitudes of teen-agers and their families all over this land, and beyond. As I bring these pages to a close, these good people seem to press forward and around to get a hearing: ministers, missionaries, chaplains, teachers; men and women in every walk of life, housewives, physicians, students; reclaimed addicts, youngsters snatched out of the grip of the asphalt jungle, grateful parents who never get tired of telling the story of what happened to "my two boys," to "our three children . . ." A typical American businessman pictures his condition and that of his family before Young Life ultimately touched them all. The quality of trust now exhibited in the face of trial—such as a current bout with tuberculosis—is such a far cry from the pathetic efforts of the drunkard of years past to escape from futility!

All such testimonies continue to come to me from every side. And yet I have all along resisted the temptation to argue from them, this manner and type of approach having long been discredited by misuse and exaggeration. The witness of positive and enduring results a thousandfold multiplied is there, nevertheless.

I started out by saying that teen-agers were not popular in America today. The burden of these pages is that the tide has turned.

To God alone be the glory.